PERSISTENCE
AND
PERSPECTIVE

FRANKLIN TEMPLETON
INVESTMENTS

THE FIRST SIXTY YEARS

PERSISTENCE AND PERSPECTIVE

FRANKLIN TEMPLETON INVESTMENTS

THE FIRST SIXTY YEARS

By Eric John Abrahamson

&

Grant Alger

Vantage Point Historical
Services, Inc.

Foreword by Charles B. Johnson

To the memory of Harmon E. Burns,
who brought intelligence, insight and character
to everything he did.
(1945-2006)

Published by Franklin Resources, Inc.
One Franklin Parkway, San Mateo, CA 94403-1906, USA

© 2007 by Franklin Resources, Inc. All rights reserved.

PHOTO CREDITS
Except for the following, all photos provided by the Franklin Templeton Archives:
p. xii, Duplessis, National Archives and Records Administration (NARA); p. xv, NARA;
p. 2, OWI from Galloway, NARA; p. 11, Don Phelan, United Press International (UPI), NARA; p. 16, UPI, NARA;
p. 22, Courtesy NYC Municipal Archives; p. 29, Richard Stoker Archives; p. 30, Tom Cotter Archives;
p. 31, *The Stock Market Magazine*; p. 35, Courtesy Harold Jacob; p. 36, Getty Images; p. 62, NARA; p. 64, NARA;
p. 72, NSCC; p. 87, Tom Cotter Archives; p. 89, FEMA News Photo, NARA; p. 101, John Galbraith Archives;
p. 106, Courtesy *Institutional Investor*; p. 112, Courtesy *Investment Advisor*; p. 117, photo: Chris Buck, text reprinted by permission
of *Fortune* magazine. FORTUNE is a registered trademark of FORTUNE magazine, a division of Time, Inc.; p. 120, Getty Images;
p. 140, Getty Images; p. 144, photo: Bill Reitzel, text reprinted by permission of *Money* magazine; p. 160, *Working Woman* magazine;
p. 164, Getty Images; p. 165, photo: Evan Kafka, text reprinted by permission of *Forbes* magazine © Forbes Media LLC.

CHART SOURCES
p. 28, "California's Population Boom," U.S. Census; p. 33, "The Go-Go Years," www.dowjones.com;
p. 54, "The Hard Years," Franklin Resources, Inc., Annual Reports, 1971–1975;
p. 68, "Mutual Funds Take Off," Investment Company Institute (ICI), "Highlights of ICI Accomplishments and Activities, 1940–2005,"
Washington, D.C.: ICI, 2006; p. 76, "Franklin's Growing Team," Franklin Resources, Inc., Annual Reports, 1983–1988;
p. 85, "Franklin Funds Take Off," Franklin Resources, Inc., Annual Reports, 1982–1987;
p. 150, "Franklin's Response to Changing Demand," Franklin Resources, Inc., Form 10-K 1987 and Annual Report 1998;
p. 151, "Franklin Templeton's Team," Franklin Resources, Inc., Annual Reports, 1992–1999;
p. 193, "Global Expansion," Franklin Resources, Inc., Annual Reports 1998–2004;
p. 198, "Franklin Templeton's Global Footprint," Investor Relations, Franklin Resources, Inc., June 30, 2006, PowerPoint presentation;
p. 201, "Historic Increase in BEN Stock," Franklin Resources, Inc., Investor Relations.

Design by Raul Cabra, Cabra Diseño, San Francisco

Printed in Canada

ISBN: 978-0-9796389-0-9

Contents

Foreword

The impetus for this book was my desire to tell the stories of the people who have shaped Franklin Templeton Investments over the past 60 years. The company was founded, built and continues to thrive on the hard work and persistence of people who share a core set of values.

At one stage of our careers we all learned, one way or another, the importance of putting clients first, building relationships, achieving quality results and working with integrity. Telling our stories is perhaps the most effective way to illustrate how these fundamental principles have been woven into the fabric of our corporate culture.

My father, Rupert H. Johnson, Sr., taught me many enduring lessons about self-reliance, the value of money and, of course, frugality. My father built a retail securities brokerage firm in the 1930s and 1940s. He had the mail clerk completely slice open every used envelope and make them into notepads. Occasionally, some salesmen would think that this was beneath them. As you will learn in the pages that follow, my father espoused the virtues of Benjamin Franklin and encouraged me and my siblings to study Franklin's *Autobiography.*

Another great teacher was Clary Anderson, my high school football coach in Montclair, New Jersey. Among other things, he imparted essential lessons about teamwork. We won a state championship my senior year, not because of any one person's star power but because Coach Anderson was so adept at building a team and getting people to work together. As the leader of this company, I always felt that a significant part of my job was to find good people and make it possible for them to do great work.

The values we learn from the most influential people in our lives, like my father and Coach Anderson, shape the decisions that we make and the way we conduct ourselves, not just in business but in our personal lives as well. My wife, Ann, and I have been together since even before I joined the company in 1957. She is a wonderful partner, mother and friend, and any success of mine also belongs to her. Ann, too, has been a teacher for me, and we have endeavored to instill in our children what we have gleaned from life. Similarly, it is my hope that those of us who have enjoyed positions of leadership at Franklin Templeton will pass the core values along to the next generation of leaders and employees, who I am confident will take the company to new heights.

I am frequently asked to give advice to young people starting out in business. On such occasions my thoughts turn to the words of Calvin Coolidge that are engraved on a plaque that has been hanging on my office wall for many years:

Persistence . . .

Press on. Nothing in the world can take the place of persistence. Talent will not; nothing is more common than unsuccessful men with talent. Genius will not; unrewarded genius is almost a proverb. Education will not; the world is full of educated derelicts. Persistence and determination alone are omnipotent.

Persistence often necessitates sacrifice. When I was a teenager I traded idle hours for the practice field, but any athlete will tell you that a few bruises and bumps are a fair swap to be on a championship team. In the early days of this company we all made sacrifices. It was a risky proposition, we were not guaranteed success, we could have made more money working for somebody else, and we sometimes surrendered family and social time for the good of the business. But it was worth it to be part of a winning team.

In 1787, as delegates signed the U.S. Constitution in Independence Hall in Philadelphia, Benjamin Franklin pointed to the president's chair, which had a sun painted on it. He said, "I have often, in the course of this session, looked at that sun without being able to tell whether it was rising or setting; but now, at length, I have the happiness to know that it is a rising and not a setting sun."

Collecting and reviewing our historical material for this project over the past year has been an interesting exercise and, at times, I could relate to Franklin's perspective here. When I was in the thick of running the business, it was often difficult to view our company with an objective eye but, looking back, I certainly feel privileged to have been a part of all that we have accomplished.

If you are reading this book, then it is likely that you are an employee, a client or a friend of Franklin Templeton Investments; and I would like to thank you for your ongoing support. Please enjoy this chronicle of what I imagine to be just the beginning chapters of our story.

CHARLES B. JOHNSON
CHAIRMAN

Prologue

*Your history is so remarkable, that if you do not give it, somebody
else will certainly give it; and perhaps so as nearly to do as
much harm, as your own management of the thing might do good.*

- BENJAMIN VAUGHN TO BENJAMIN FRANKLIN,
PARIS, JANUARY 31, 1783

In January 1783 Benjamin Franklin received a letter from an old friend. At the age of 77, Franklin was the elder statesman of the American Revolution and the new government of the United States. He was also the new country's richest citizen, having earned and saved his wealth over a lifetime rather than receiving it by inheritance or privilege. The letter from Benjamin Vaughn urged him to finish writing his autobiography for the sake of future generations.

Franklin hesitated before acting on Vaughn's suggestion. Autobiography always risks the appearance of vanity, and Franklin had long struggled to come to terms with his natural pride. Twelve years earlier, in a letter to his son, he suggested that it was good to be proud of one's accomplishments. "Most people dislike vanity in others . . . ," he wrote, "but I give it fair quarter wherever I meet with it, being persuaded that it is often productive of good to the possessor & to others that are within his sphere of action."

Statesman, scientist and author, Benjamin Franklin was also a successful investor who inspired many young entrepreneurs with his *Autobiography*. In 1947 Rupert H. Johnson, Sr., named his mutual fund company after Franklin.

Vaughn told Franklin that the story of his life could be of use to future generations. It would guide others along the path to prosperity and well-being. Franklin's life affirmed the Enlightenment idea that individuals could shape their own destiny. By educating themselves and persevering even during the darkest times, they could move from poverty to prosperity and from obscurity to leadership.

Vaughn argued that Franklin's lifelong efforts to articulate and then discipline himself to a code of conduct offered an extraordinary self-help lesson to a younger generation striving to follow a virtuous path guided by an internal moral compass. The full tale of Franklin's life, wrote Vaughn, would suggest to readers that they should act with the long run in mind to avoid the "torment of foolish impatience."

Fortunately for future generations, Franklin followed Vaughn's advice. His *Autobiography* became an American classic, read by generations of youth hoping to improve themselves by study and become financially independent through hard work and thrift. More than 100 years later, one of the young men who read Franklin's book and took his advice to heart was Rupert H. Johnson, Sr.

THE WAY TO WALL STREET

Rupert H. Johnson, Sr., was born in 1899 in Jones County, Texas. His childhood was characterized by frontier entrepreneurship, the recreations and labors of country life, and the social excitements of a large extended family. His father, Albert Washington Johnson, was the son of a Baptist minister and a strict disciplinarian, a man of exceptional energy with an

A HABIT OF VIRTUE

As a young man, Benjamin Franklin listed 13 virtues that he associated with good character, then focused on each of these virtues one week at a time.

The list included temperance, silence, order, resolution, frugality, industry, sincerity, justice, moderation, cleanliness, tranquility, chastity and humility.

On the virtue of frugality, he wrote: "Make no expense but to do good to others or yourself, in other words, waste nothing."

appetite for business ventures. In Anson, Texas, he owned an ice plant, the local bank, the town's central waterworks, the electric light plant and a 640-acre farm. His son Rupert described him as "one of the best businessmen I have ever known."

⟞Like many children in frontier communities, Rupert grew up quickly. At the age of 15 he left home to attend Hardin-Simmons University, a Baptist college in Abilene, Texas. When the United States entered World War I in 1917, he joined the army and earned a Purple Heart on the battlefield in France. He received an appointment to West Point where he excelled as an athlete. He boxed, played baseball and basketball, and rode on the polo team. After graduating from West Point in 1921, he became an officer in the infantry, but stayed for only two years.

⟞Rupert was eager to get to Wall Street. He took a job in a bank, but, according to his son Charlie, "He decided that selling securities was a very good profession because the harder you worked, the better your rewards. And he certainly wasn't one to dodge hard work." Joining the firm of Harris Forbes & Co., Rupert began selling bonds. In 1927 he started his own retail brokerage firm. With a partner and backing from his partner's wealthy father, Rupert launched Stenzel, Johnson and Company in December 1927.

⟞During the late 1920s, thousands of Americans hoping to "get rich quick" rushed into the stock market—ignoring Benjamin Franklin's advice to

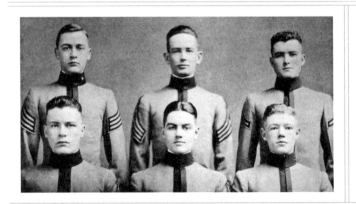

Rupert H. Johnson, Sr., (back row, right) received an appointment to West Point after earning a Purple Heart during World War I. After graduating, he was eager to work on Wall Street.

build one's fortune over a lifetime. But this was not yet a "people's market." By some estimates, less than 2.5 percent of the American populace owned securities by 1928. Much of the money being thrown into the stock market came from corporations that were flush with profits and found equity investing a more profitable use of cash reserves than capital improvements. Commercial banks, corporations and wealthy individuals channeled funds into the call money market

in 1928. The availability of this easy credit allowed brokers to finance their customers' margin purchases of stock. By 1929, loans to brokers, dealers and individual investors totaled $8.3 billion.

    The first investment companies came into being during these good times on Wall Street. Massachusetts Investment Trust (MIT) was formed in 1924 (this company later became MFS). As the excitement on Wall Street accelerated in the late 1920s, investors eagerly bought shares in the new mutual funds. By 1928, 55,000 Americans owned funds. A year later, that number exploded to 525,000. Some investors traded shares in these new funds in a way that foreshadowed the Internet trading craze that would occur again more than 70 years later—they weren't always sure what they were investing in, but felt certain they would make money.

    During the fall of 1929, uncertainty began to color the stock markets. Prices declined steadily in September and early October. A feverish sell-off that started on October 23 accelerated on the 24th, a day that would become known as Black Thursday. To prevent a complete collapse, banks and investment houses stepped in and began buying. Bankers hoped that the worst was over, but it was not. When the market opened again on Monday, panic selling accelerated. The next day, subsequently known as Black Tuesday, the market continued to plummet. By the time the market closed, stocks had lost nearly 50 percent of their August values. Tens of thousands of people lost their life savings, and many Americans suddenly had a much more negative view of Wall Street.

RULES MAKE
A NEW
INDUSTRY

Sweeping legislation passed during the Great Depression shaped the mutual fund and securities industries in the United States. Among the most important laws:

The Securities Act of 1933, or "Truth in Securities Act," reorganized the nation's financial markets and provided greater government oversight of the banking and securities industries.

The Securities Exchange Act, passed in 1934, created the Securities and Exchange Commission (SEC) to oversee the industry.

The Maloney Act, passed in 1938, led to the birth of the National Association of Securities Dealers (NASD).

The Investment Company Act, passed in 1940, governs the operation of mutual funds in the United States. The Act requires investment companies to provide investors with accurate information and operate in the interest of shareholders. It also regulates their capital structures and prohibits self-dealing transactions.

The crash led to a major restructuring of the brokerage industry. Many brokers, including Rupert's partner, left the business. Rupert persevered, renaming the company "R. H. Johnson & Co." To fund operations, he put a second mortgage on his home. He cut personal expenses "to bedrock." Renting the family home, he moved with his wife and children into an apartment. His personal sacrifices paid off. In 1932 he made a profit of $25,000. He started hiring salesmen to sell bonds and began to expand his business. Headquartered at 64 Wall Street, R. H. Johnson & Co. opened offices in Buffalo and then expanded throughout New England and into Pennsylvania. During the 1930s and 1940s, Rupert had more than 200 salesmen selling bonds, equities and mutual funds.

SECURITIES SALESMEN

We are interested in employing securities salesmen in or near the offices where we operate or in other centers where such men may be now established. We would consider opening offices in other cities where a man might become manager for us. We are also conducting a school for securities salesmen where we train men without previous knowledge of the securities business. After 3 to 6 months training they are allowed to sell under supervision of experienced men.

Inquiries to be addressed to Mr. Markell of our New York office.

R. H. JOHNSON & CO.
Established 1927
INVESTMENT SECURITIES
64 Wall Street, New York 5

BOSTON   PHILADELPHIA

Troy   Albany   Buffalo   Syracuse   Pittsburgh   Dallas   Wilkes Barre
Washington   Baltimore   Springfield   Woonsocket

In 1946, Rupert H. Johnson, Sr., recruited salesmen to help expand his broker/dealer business. The mutual fund business he launched the following year was intended to be a sideline.

In the meantime, Congress and President Franklin Delano Roosevelt began to change the rules that governed the marketplace for investing, passing a series of laws that would frame the industry for the rest of the century. In particular, the Investment Company Act of 1940 eliminated some of the uncertainty in the mutual fund business by providing new protections for fund investors.

Rupert had long been intrigued by mutual funds. When his friend Chauncey Waddell and Cam Reed launched the United Funds in 1941, Rupert considered creating his own fund but put the idea on hold at the outbreak of World War II. When the war ended, Rupert founded Franklin Distributors, Inc., a mutual fund management company, on November 18, 1947. He branched away from the dominant industry approach at the time. Instead of organizing just a single fund, he followed a more ambitious strategy of developing a series of five funds, known as Franklin Custodian Funds, to satisfy the needs of different investors with different goals and interests. By the end of 1948,

A successful entrepreneur, Rupert H. Johnson, Sr., had more than 200 salesmen selling bonds, equities and mutual funds after World War II. He retired in 1956 to focus on his own investments and to travel.

THE FIRST FRANKLIN FUNDS

Ten days after he organized the mutual fund management company of Franklin Distributors, Rupert H. Johnson founded Franklin Custodian Funds on November 28, 1947. The company began offering shares to investors four months later, on March 25, 1948. Franklin Custodian Funds gave investors five different fund options: Franklin Common Stock Fund, Franklin Preferred Stock Fund, Franklin Bond Fund, Franklin Utilities Fund and Franklin Income Fund (a balanced fund).

these five funds had a total of $400,000 under management.

Rupert named the company after Benjamin Franklin because Franklin epitomized the ideas of frugality and prudence when it came to saving and investing. He anticipated that investors in the funds would be inspired by Franklin's convictions about saving and investments. Indeed, he believed so much in Franklin's philosophy that as his children grew up, he offered each of them $50 to read Franklin's *Autobiography*. His son Charlie took both the $50 and the book's messages to heart.

CHAPTER
I

Franklin's
Wall Street Era

After taking over Franklin in 1957, Charlie Johnson focused on building the company's relationships with brokers. The company's offices at 99 Wall Street overlooked America's financial district.

Opposite: Looking to the east, an aerial view of Wall Street and the financial district in New York City, 1950.

Wall Street Era

*Energy and persistence
conquer all things.*

- BENJAMIN FRANKLIN

Charlie Johnson
1949

First Lieutenant Charles (Charlie) B. Johnson boarded the train for the six-hour trip to Paris in February 1957. A cold war soldier, he had left his wife, Ann, and eight-month-old son, Chuck, back in their quarters on an American base in West Germany. Charlie was going to see his father for the first time in almost a year. "The Old Gent," as Rupert called himself, had sailed from New York to London on an ocean liner. From England he crossed the Channel and took the train to Paris.

Later in Paris, as the two men stood waiting for the maitre d' at Maxim's to seat them, the father-son resemblance must have been visible to the diners at other tables. In middle age, Rupert was a vigorous man who kept in shape by walking. Unlike most people in his generation, he did not smoke cigarettes, although he enjoyed an occasional cigar. Three decades earlier, he had been one of only a handful of men to letter in four varsity sports at West Point. The self-discipline that helped him survive the trenches of World War I and got him through West Point was still reflected in his character. In the style of former U.S. President Teddy Roosevelt, Rupert had contracted with a world-famous guide and now was headed to East Africa to hunt elephants, giraffes, lions and rhinos.

Charlie, at age 24, was similarly fit. He had the chest and shoulders of a front-line football player. Growing up in a working-class New Jersey neighborhood, he had played football for Montclair High School and helped his team win the state championship in his senior year. Success on the gridiron helped him get into Yale University, where he was a member of the Reserve Officers' Training Corps (ROTC).

In his senior year at Yale, Charlie played on the rugby team and traveled to Bermuda over spring break for a competition. In Bermuda, he met Ann Lutes, who was vacationing there with a group from her all-girls school. Three years younger than Charlie, Ann also lived in New Jersey, 30 minutes from where Charlie had grown up. Her father had worked as

After graduating from Yale, Charlie Johnson served in the U.S. Army in West Germany. As the end of his service approached, he made plans to relaunch the mutual fund company founded by his father in 1947.

an electrical engineer for the Bell Telephone Company of New York City, but died while Ann was still a young girl. By the time she met Charlie, Ann had lost her mother as well.

The courtship between Charlie and Ann that began in Bermuda continued back in the States. After Charlie's graduation from college and Ann's graduation from high school, Charlie went to Europe. When he returned to the United States, he and Ann continued to date. "Charlie is a caretaker," says Ann. "I was the perfect person for him. I could see him thinking, 'Here's this girl with no parents. I have to take care of her.'" In the fall, Charlie took Ann to college at Bryn Mawr near Philadelphia and made sure she was settled in the dorm. Over the next six months, he worked for his father on Wall Street and began learning the securities and mutual fund business, while Ann started her studies, hoping to go on to medical school after she graduated. They became engaged over Thanksgiving and married in March 1955.

Now a grown man with his own family, Charlie was still a little on his guard around his father. Rupert had a habit of testing and interrogating his children at the dinner table and was forever imparting moral lessons, holding up Benjamin Franklin as a role model. Rupert's stern character had been shaped not just by Franklin's moral views, but also by Baptist country traditions and the disciplines demanded by World War I, West Point and Wall Street. While influenced by his father's virtues and values, Charlie also had his mother's natural comfort and grace. According to one family member, he "did not have the abruptness or the brusqueness" that many people associated with his father.

That February night in 1957, as the two men dined on the world-famous cuisine at Maxim's, they caught up on family matters and discussed the future. Rupert had wrapped up his business affairs in New York. Charlie's older brother, Andy, a recent graduate of the University of Virginia's law school, had joined Rupert's former partners and relaunched his father's brokerage business under the name of Dewey, King and Johnson. The Franklin Life Insurance Company, based in Springfield,

Illinois, had expressed an interest in buying the management of Franklin Custodian Funds, the mutual fund side of Rupert's business. Charlie told his father he wanted to take it over instead.

≈Charlie was looking forward to going home and getting started. The American economy was growing. More and more people were joining the ranks of the middle class. Charlie saw vast opportunity and had plans to expand the fledgling company his father had founded.

BACK HOME ON WALL STREET

With only about $2.5 million in assets under management, Franklin was a tiny company in a young industry when Charlie took the reins in 1957. Other fund firms, including Fidelity, Dreyfus and Wellington funds, were all much bigger than Franklin and had a much easier time selling their funds.

≈To build Franklin's business, Charlie focused on brokers. To win their confidence, he emphasized Franklin's independence from the brokerage firm that had once belonged to his father. Not long after returning to Wall Street in April 1957, he had workers build a wall to separate his offices from the brokerage firm of Dewey, King and Johnson. He had the workers cut a separate entrance as well, and on the door he painted in gold-leaf letters: "Franklin Custodian Funds."

≈With $10,000 in initial capital, Charlie's strategy for growing the business was straightforward: Call on dealers, make them aware of the advantages of Franklin Custodian Funds and assure them that they would receive good service and honest information. He relied on the *Red Book,* a guide to brokers, to assemble lists of marketing calls. Then he packed his car and hit the road. His first trip was to upstate New York, where he drove from Albany to Buffalo, and on subsequent trips he called on mutual fund brokers in Pennsylvania, New Jersey and Long Island.

≈In the beginning Charlie was the company. Ann sewed the curtains for the windows in the office. To answer the phones, write checks and handle the business back on Wall Street, Charlie recruited Charlotte O'Connell, who had worked at his father's brokerage firm and

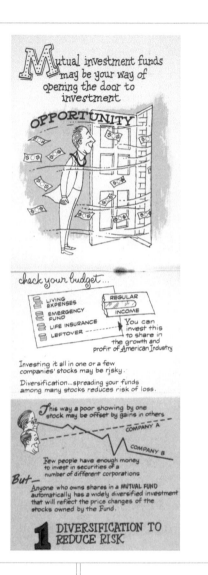

Mutual funds were still a relatively uncommon investment vehicle in the 1950s. Industry brochures such as *7 Reasons for Investing in Mutual Funds* helped brokers discuss the benefits of diversification and professional management.

at Dewey, King and Johnson. Charlie also hired Marion Zahar to do bookkeeping part-time. By hiring people with whom he had some history, Charlie felt he could leave the office on sales calls and trust that business was being handled properly while he was away. This was the beginning of a lifetime pattern, in which Charlie made hiring decisions and gave people a great deal of responsibility based on his knowledge of their character and work ethic.

On the road and face to face with brokers, Charlie's challenge was to explain the advantages of mutual funds. He created a brochure that described the funds and provided an overview of their performance. Of the five Franklin funds that Charlie managed in 1957, the utilities fund was the most interesting to many brokers.

Other companies offered similar "specialty" mutual funds in steel, railroad stocks and other industries, but only Franklin had a fund focused on utilities. "Half the electric utilities raised their dividends every year," Charlie remembers, which made the fund "a very compelling story" over the long term. Franklin Utilities Fund's solid record "got us off the ground" in terms of sales and underscored Charlie's commitment to long-term performance.

Traveling and calling on brokers gave Charlie a better understanding of the market. He learned how to get the attention of brokers, and education became a key part of the Franklin strategy. One of the most important messages he delivered to brokers was that an investment in mutual funds could provide a better savings vehicle than whole life insurance, which was a very popular savings vehicle at the time. "As a practical matter," says Charlie, "these life insurance policies delivered returns to people of about 1 or 2 percent a year. It was really a very poor savings product."

An alternative strategy for investors, popularized in the late 1950s, replaced whole life policies with term life insurance and invested the cash values in mutual funds. Automatic investment plans (also known as contractual plans or installment plans) made it easy for middle-class investors to leverage their savings without having to invest large amounts of money all at once. Charlie launched Franklin's own automatic investment plan in 1959.

⁀One of the brokers Charlie called on in the late 1950s was Bill Lippman. Based in New Jersey, Lippman was already selling mutual funds from Dreyfus, Oppenheimer and Founders. When Charlie called on him, Lippman was impressed. "He was a very likable guy who knew his subject. He was very good at what he did." After meeting Charlie, Lippman added Franklin's funds to the range of products he offered investors.

⁀Like many new brokers in the 1950s, Lippman worked to build his client base by cold-calling. He focused on middle-class businesspeople. "I would get a list of the plumbers in the community," he says, "or the undertakers or whatever group I thought should listen to me." If he reached one person out of 10 who wouldn't hang up or be rude to him, Lippman thought he was doing well. These were the people who were investing their savings in whole life policies. They were also the people who Lippman and Charlie believed should be in mutual funds.

⁀Persistence, perseverance and a thick skin were essential because Franklin was swimming against the tide in the late 1950s and early 1960s. Insurance companies dominated the middle-class investing markets, and firms that did sell funds often preferred to work with older, more established mutual fund companies. Many large broker/dealers, including Merrill Lynch, banned the sale of all mutual funds. Charlie Merrill was concerned that if mutual funds became too popular, promoting a buy-and-hold approach to investing, they would diminish the trading activity that was the broker's bread and butter. What Merrill didn't appreciate was that fund managers would be as active as individual investors, or more so, and Merrill Lynch and the other brokers had an opportunity to grow their business by serving them.

⁀In contrast to a broker like Merrill, Charlie Johnson liked the structure of the mutual fund industry because it was less dependent on the constant effort to get investors to make new transactions. He also

A FAMILY WATCHES THE DEBATE BETWEEN PRESIDENTIAL
CANDIDATES JOHN F. KENNEDY AND RICHARD M. NIXON
ON SEPTEMBER 26, 1960. TELEVISION WAS ONE OF MANY
NEW CONSUMER PRODUCTS THAT HELPED FUEL ECONOMIC
GROWTH IN POSTWAR AMERICA. POSTWAR PROSPERITY ALSO
ENCOURAGED AMERICA'S GROWING MIDDLE CLASS TO SAVE
FOR COLLEGE AND RETIREMENT.

Franklin Almanac

The Almanac is published by Franklin Distributors, wholesale distributors of Franklin Custodian Funds. It is for dealers only and not for distribution to the investing public.

November 3, 1958	Vol. I Issue 40

RELIABILITY

...... By Elmer G. Leterman

"He Delivers!"

In just those two words you get a clear picture of a salesman who has created positive satisfaction and powerful loyalty in his customers.

No empty big talk from such a salesman! No uncertainties. No delays. No disappointments. No excuses. NO ALIBIS.

Few things in this world can win people to you more solidly than promises that are kept like that, right on the dot.

KEEP YOUR PROMISES and YOU WILL KEEP YOUR FRIENDS

Promises that are kept mean customers that are kept...but never promise what you can't deliver.

know a man whom I consider to be one of the "sweetest talking" salesmen I've ever met. can talk up anything from toilet supplies to luxury cars so persuasively, so convincingly, that you're almost sure the birds in the trees stop singing to listen to him.

But he has one big trouble. He gets so carried away by his own eloquence that in his own mind nothing seems impossible, nothing seems too good to be true or too impractical to promise.

As a consequence, he will promise anything.

Then, in the cold gray morning after such a binge of intoxication with the sound of his own voice, he too often has to creep back to his prospect with another kind of bird. He has to eat crow. Soberly, and with all kinds of apologies and alibis, he has to confess that he promised too much.

JUST 1% MORE

We were all recently startled by the news that the U.S. had a rocket on its way to the moon - 220,000 miles away. As the rocket progressed I waited anxiously to see if it would make it. Later in the day I learned it had travelled only 79,000 miles and was on its way back. This 79,000 seemed a far cry from the 220,000 miles needed, but all the scientists praised how close we had come. It was a few days later that I learned that we had failed by only 1% in our effort. If the speed of the rocket had been only 1% more it would have travelled the extra 141,000 miles necessary to reach the moon.

Sounds incredible doesn't it? Only 1% more speed... Yet it points out a lesson in selling that only a little more effort can carry you a long, long way ahead. The fellow who constently puts out that extra 1% is the one who heads the sales ladder at the end of the year.

FRANKLIN DISTRIBUTORS, INC.
Telephone HAnover 2-0810

64 Wall Street, New York, N.Y.
Teletype NY 1-4073

THE *Franklin Almanac* PROVIDED SALES ADVICE AND INSPIRATION TO BROKERS. CHARLIE JOHNSON AND OTHERS AT FRANKLIN USED THE MIMEOGRAPHED PUBLICATION TO KEEP THE FRANKLIN FUNDS IN FRONT OF BROKERS AND TO HELP BROKERS BUILD THEIR BUSINESS.

believed it was better for the average investor who benefited from the pooling of risk and minimal transaction costs.

Knowing he faced an uphill battle against the large brokerage firms and insurance industry, Charlie focused on keeping the Franklin name in front of brokers. In 1958 he launched a newsletter called the *Franklin Almanac*. Borrowing Benjamin Franklin's portrait and the style of Poor Richard's homilies, the *Franklin Almanac* provided motivational advice with tips on how to understand customers, perspectives on the importance of saving and investing, strategies for making a sale and investment tips to develop a diversified, balanced portfolio. The weekly newsletter kept the Franklin name on brokers' desks.

During these early years, Charlie and Ann and their growing family lived in a working-class neighborhood in Montclair, New Jersey, near where Charlie had grown up. They bought a house that needed work. In the little spare time he had from the business, Charlie made repairs and painted. When it was ready and Chuck was old enough for kindergarten, they sold the house at a profit and bought another fixer-upper. Charlie replaced the kitchen floor. Ann wallpapered the living room.

Family life was shaped in part by the disciplines of the business. "We took one night of the weekend to take the children out," Ann remembers, "and then we would go out the other night." At one point, Charlie started to play golf, but it took too much time away from home and work, so he stopped. Six days a week Charlie commuted to Manhattan. "He worked from seven to seven," Ann remembers. But the long hours paid off. By the early 1960s, Franklin was growing.

Increasingly, Charlie found that he needed help. He hired Roger Hanson, a friend who had worked for Smith Barney and trained as a securities salesman, to work as a wholesaler. Sometimes at night, as Charlie headed home for New Jersey, he stopped at his sister Dorothy's house to drop off typing and then picked up the work the following morning on his way to the office. Like most entrepreneurs, he made use of the talents and resources that were readily available, and he invested as much as possible back into the business. "We had three children and a house," Ann remembers, "but his secretary brought home more than he did." Charlie had a vision of where he wanted to go, but struggled every day just to keep up with the day-to-day demands of the business and managing the Franklin funds.

BENEFITING FROM MARKET GROWTH

Charlie Johnson's first year at the helm of Franklin was inauspicious, as net industry assets declined by 4 percent. Growth picked up in 1958, and Franklin benefited from the improvements in the market, as did others who were trying to build their businesses. Some of those entrepreneurs would be important to the future of Franklin.

John Templeton, for example, had entered the mutual fund industry in 1954 when he established Templeton Growth Fund. A Yale alum like Charlie, he had started on Wall Street in 1934, then worked for

Templeton Growth Fund logo 1954

a short time at a Texas oil company. In 1940 he bought a small investment advisory concern that became Templeton, Dobbrow and Vance, Inc. (TDV). Templeton Growth Fund had two unusual features. First, it was incorporated in Canada as a way to reduce the tax liability of its shareholders, since Canada then lacked a capital gains tax. Second, it was one of the earliest global funds that focused on investing in the "securities of companies deriving income from outside the United States."

In 1956 Templeton joined with marketing consultant William Damroth to launch Nucleonics, Chemistry and Electronics Fund, a specialty fund that reflected Templeton's lifelong interest in science and technology. With investor interest in specialty funds rising in the late 1950s, Templeton Damroth's new fund grew dramatically. Hoping to raise capital to finance more growth, Templeton then made a bold move to accelerate his company's growth.

In this era, mutual fund management companies rarely became public corporations. As a result, they were denied access to the public markets to raise capital to grow. A series of court decisions during the late 1950s, however, had clarified the provisions of the Investment Company Act of 1940 and upheld the right of fund management companies to "go public." With five funds under management and total net investments of over $66 million in 1959, John Templeton seized the opportunity to raise capital, and Templeton Damroth joined a sudden surge of fund firms that went public at this time.

Charlie Johnson may have wished for a similar opportunity to raise capital, but in 1959 Franklin Custodian Funds had less than $4 million in assets under management. Soon, the company would also face new challenges in the regulatory environment.

A CHANGING REGULATORY CLIMATE

In the fall of 1961, Charlie had his first encounter with examiners from the Securities and Exchange Commission (SEC). He was out calling on brokers when the agents came into the office. "It was a routine thing," Charlie remembers, but the investigation revealed that "our accounting was not as good as it should have been." Working hard to build the business, Charlie was wearing a lot of hats and had delegated most of the accounting to a bookkeeper and auditors who came in periodically to produce financial statements.

That fall, the company was late producing its annual report. Like many mutual funds in this era, Franklin used an outside transfer agent to maintain the records of purchases, sales and account balances of its fund investors. "When the SEC came in, we had some accounting errors and some differences with the books and records of our custodian and transfer agent, the First National Bank of New Jersey," says Charlie. These accounting issues led to an SEC decision to withhold approval for the renewal of Franklin's prospectus until the company could complete its audited financial statements.

The delay proved expensive. While the auditors were working on a revised annual report, the stock market was in serious decline, dropping from 900 to less than 600 in a matter of months. Franklin compounded its problems by continuing to sell the funds in anticipation of the SEC's decision. "That was a judgment failure," Charlie says. "We should have just bitten the bullet. But we didn't want the brokers to stop selling the funds." Soon, the delay over the approval forced Franklin to cancel these "when issued" sales, and brokers had to return the commissions they had earned. "Essentially, that put us out of business," Charlie recalls.

The crisis had both short-term and long-term effects. It interrupted sales and the flow of revenues, while threatening to erode the work Charlie had done to build relationships with brokers. "Out of sight, out of mind," Charlie says. "They would move on to doing other things."

To resolve the issues with the SEC, Charlie hired additional accounting staff and retained David Schenker as special counsel. Schenker

In 1962 the Dow Jones Industrial Average lost one-third of its value in a matter of months. Many young traders on the floor of the New York Stock Exchange learned a powerful lesson about market cycles from this mini-crash.

had served as chief counsel to the SEC's Investment Trust Study and had been the principal author of the Investment Company Act. On his desk he had the pen that President Franklin Roosevelt had used to sign the Act. The SEC had demanded that Franklin not only get its accounting in order, but also recruit a new board of directors for the funds.

⤳Schenker helped Charlie establish a new board, including Edmund Kerr, Philip Russell, George Zolatar and others who had standing on Wall Street and would build confidence with regulators and investors. Paul Windels, Jr., for example, a graduate of Princeton and Harvard Law School, had been a federal prosecutor of securities frauds in the mid-1950s and New York SEC regional administrator from 1956 to 1961. This board marked the beginning of a major change in the industry. Unlike other fund boards of the era, Franklin's new board was totally independent of the management staff of the company.

⤳In this same period, Charlie also hired industry veteran Sam Morse to manage Franklin's back-office operations. Morse had started working on Wall Street during the depths of the Depression. In three decades on Wall Street, he had gained invaluable experience dealing with NASD

PHILIP RUSSELL

When Franklin Custodian Funds had to remake its board of directors in 1962, Charlie Johnson looked for individuals with strong reputations and a deep knowledge of the industry. Phil Russell was an ideal candidate.

Russell had recently retired from the Mutual Insurance Company, where he had been the chief investment officer. An engineering graduate of the Massachusetts Institute of Technology (MIT), he was smart and well connected within the industry.

Russell became the independent chairman of the Franklin Custodian Funds board in the late 1960s, and remained in that position until July 1983. He provided a critical sounding board on issues of investment strategy and offered encouragement to Charlie and other senior executives through the hard years in the 1970s. When he left the company in 1983, Franklin had finally turned a corner and entered a long period of prosperous growth.

RICHARD
STOKER

Dick Stoker grew up in California, the son of a crop-dusting entrepreneur in El Centro. His mother was Rupert H. Johnson, Sr.'s sister and Charlie and Rupert, Jr.'s aunt.

When Stoker first started working for Franklin in September 1961, he had to learn everything from the ground up. In 1967, during the go-go years, Stoker left Franklin to join the fast-growing Shareholders Management Company in Los Angeles. With the stock market crash in 1970, however, he came back to Franklin.

Through the 1970s, he was routinely invited to speak to groups of investors about strategies for investing. The seminars earned him the nickname of "Stoker the Broker."

and SEC concerns. As Charlie drafted new sales literature for the funds, Morse edited the material so it would win approval from the regulators. But it took until May 1962 for the company to reissue its prospectus. In the meantime, Franklin kept pushing forward. "Charlie's philosophy was just the same as his father's," recalls one longtime employee. "You work hard. You play by the rules. And you never quit, you persevere."

GATHERING THE TALENT

A rock-and-roll performer in college, Dick Stoker had dreams of making it in the music industry, but his uncle, Rupert Johnson, had other ideas. Stoker had landed a job as an usher at CBS Television in 1960 shortly after graduating from college. Between episodes of Red Skelton or Jack Benny, he brought water to the stars. Over Thanksgiving dinner, just weeks after John Kennedy defeated Richard Nixon for the presidency of the United States in 1960, Rupert suggested that his nephew go into mutual funds. Stoker wasn't sure about the idea of moving to New York, but his wife, who was from the East Coast, had had enough of California. The next summer, they rented a home in the quintessential postwar American suburb of Levittown, New York, and Stoker joined Franklin in September.

Stoker became part of a very small, hands-on team. Five days a week the Franklin staff worked the broker/dealer community. Every Saturday, they printed a fresh edition of the *Franklin Almanac*, fed the printed copies into a folding machine and then stuffed the *Almanac* into envelopes, hoping Ben Franklin's sayings would help open a few more doors.

As he began to hand off some of the hats he had been wearing, Charlie looked for help on the investment side as well. Early in the 1960s, the company hired Jerry Palmieri as a portfolio manager. Palmieri's father had been a broker. "All my meals have come out of Wall Street," Palmieri says. After serving in the military, he had worked in the textile industry before joining Merrill Lynch in the mid-1950s. He worked at Merrill as a broker for five years. Wanting some experience on the institutional side of the business, he then took a position with Wood, Struthers, and Winthrop, but this firm was not growing. Palmieri went knocking on doors and called on Charlie Johnson.

There was no management training program for Palmieri. Franklin Distributors was still too small and operating on a shoestring. So Palmieri spent much of his free time at the New York Public Library on 42nd Street reading industry reviews. He became such a regular that the staff called him by name. As Charlie got busier and his confidence in Palmieri grew, he gave him more responsibility for managing investments.

In the meantime, Charlie's younger brother, Rupert H. Johnson, Jr., had been serving as an officer in the Marine Corps. With plenty of extra time onboard ships, he read about investing. Like other members of the Johnson family, he had spent many days in his teenage years boxing up sales kits for brokers, running errands to the post office and taking packages to brokers in Manhattan. When he was stationed at Camp Pendleton in Southern California, he took night courses on the mutual fund industry. "I was kind of preparing myself intellectually," he says. "I was just curious. I'd been around the business, and I just wanted to see it from the outside, from another person's perspective. I was verifying my own conclusions." When he finished his military service in

July 1965, he interviewed with a number of retail broker/dealers. But after talking to Charlie, he decided to join Franklin Distributors.

Initially, Rupert, Jr., shared an office with Jerry Palmieri. Two years later, when Dick Stoker left to join the Shareholders Management Company in Los Angeles, Rupert, Jr., became the wholesaler. "Everybody had to be a salesman in the organization," he remembers. Charlie went out and made sales presentations. Rupert wrote and helped design the sales literature for the company.

As they called on broker/dealers, the Franklin team faced stiff competition. Some organizations had their own mutual funds, and they resisted allowing independent funds the opportunity to pitch their products. "We tried to get their attention by not necessarily talking about products," says Rupert, Jr., "but by trying to increase their productivity." Persistent contact established a relationship. Gradually, some brokers became interested in the Johnsons' perspective on the economic scene and individual securities. According to Rupert, Jr., "We became a sounding board."

No matter what roles were assigned officially, however, every day at four o'clock in the afternoon, everyone manned the phones to take orders from broker/dealers. "You stopped everything you were doing, you had a calculator, and you took orders," Rupert, Jr., recalls. When the brokers called, whoever took the order would write it up on a ticket. Through the mid-1960s, Franklin Utilities Fund was the company's best performer, growing from $239,000 in 1955 to $28.7 million in 1965.

As the bull market of the late 1960s took off, Charlie and Rupert, Jr., were continually frustrated by their lack of capital or financing. While well-heeled companies like Fidelity, Dreyfus and Wellington were able to invest and grow, Franklin had to move more slowly. They wanted wholesalers to work regional markets, but couldn't afford to pay them a significant salary, so instead they had to recruit people who were willing to work on commission. Franklin had one or two people covering the entire United States while their competitors had salespeople in multiple regional markets.

IN THE LATE 1960s, THE FRANKLIN TEAM INCLUDED (L-R)
CHARLIE, JERRY PALMIERI AND RUPERT, JR. EVERYONE
WORE MULTIPLE HATS IN THE EARLY YEARS, SETTING
THE STAGE FOR THE COMPANY'S GROWTH AT THE END OF
THE DECADE.

The problems in 1962 set back Franklin's sales efforts substantially, but Charlie did not give up. Instead, he went in search of new office space to expand the staff. In May 1962, he leased offices at 99 Wall Street, a couple of blocks away from the East River. "We had a whole floor," remembers Jerry Palmieri. But the accommodations were sparse. Tom Cotter, a former California regional sales manager for the company, remembers his boss coaching him to keep clients away. "One time a dealer wanted to visit the office at 99 Wall Street, and I was told, 'Tom, it's better if he does not go

99 Wall Street

back there, because it's a very small headquarters, so it's not too impressive.'" Cotter was not the only salesperson to feel the effect of tight budgets.

As Dick Stoker got more involved with selling the funds to brokers, he became more aware of the sales strategies of other organizations. Some funds "had plenty of money, and their wholesalers had unlimited expense accounts," he recalls. Some of these larger organizations also built relationships by promising brokers trades on portfolio purchases. With its smaller size, Franklin had many fewer trades so it was tougher to compete. Stoker discovered that he had to work differently to build relationships with the brokers. "The key was to help them get new clients." Stoker provided brokers with advice on how to talk to clients about investing for the long run. When possible, he provided them with leads.

Fidelity, Dreyfus and Wellington were the biggest fund sellers in this era. In Stoker's memory, Dreyfus "owned the whole city and Long Island because they advertised the lion coming out of the subway." In some ways, however, Franklin benefited from the presence of the big firms. "They were teaching everybody about mutual funds," Stoker says. "They trailblazed for everybody." Dreyfus, for instance, would insert its prospectus into the Sunday *New York Times.* As investors became interested in mutual funds, the whole industry grew.

Without the capital to compete for brokers' attention or buy advertising in *The New York Times,* the *Franklin Almanac* continued to provide an inexpensive way to keep Franklin's name on the brokers' desks. The *Almanac* focused on meeting the brokers' needs. It gave them answers during a bad market. It gave them motivation when they were down. It kept them focused when the market was running away and the pressure was on to sell the hottest stocks.

Selling funds in the early 1960s, Dick Stoker spent a lot of time visiting brokers in the high-rises of New York. "At the top of 120 Broadway," he remembers, "I spent three weeks in one building going up and down and being thrown out by brokers on every floor. Then all of a sudden, maybe down at about the 50th floor, a guy would say come on in, what've you got? He'd be having lunch, and I'd tell him about the utilities fund." Unable to impress the guy eating lunch with fancy brochures or giveaways, Stoker relied on Franklin's essential commitment to helping brokers make money by meeting their clients' needs.

To win the brokers, Franklin paid them a generous commission. Franklin charged customers a commission of 8.75 percent, giving most of this money (7.75 percent of the purchase) to the broker. "That was a very aggressive payout," says Stoker. It reflected Charlie's strategic decision to build the business by building relationships. In the long run, this strategy

Franklin focused on building relationships with brokers in the early years. At the Miami mutual fund convention in Bal Harbour, Florida, in the early 1960s, Charlie Johnson (center) socialized with Jud Grosvenor (far left) from Eastman Dillon and Mac McDonald (far right) from Westamerica Securities and their wives.

worked well. In the short run, however, Franklin and the mutual fund industry faced some serious challenges coming out of Washington.

CONGRESS LOOKS AT THE SEC

Franklin's issues with the SEC in 1962 reflected broader regulatory changes taking place in the industry. Late in the 1950s, the growth of mutual funds raised fears among some on Wall Street that large-scale buying and selling by fund companies could distort the fluctuations of the equities markets. The SEC responded by asking the Wharton School of Finance and Commerce to undertake a comprehensive study of the industry.

For small, independent mutual fund companies, the SEC study was almost overwhelming. "They had this 100-page questionnaire," Charlie recalls, "and I'm working the office with two employees, and we have maybe $4 million in assets at that time." Hoping Franklin was small enough that it could escape the paperwork, Charlie applied to the SEC for an exemption, but the request was not granted. "For a while it took half of my time," Charlie says.

The payoff for Charlie and the industry came when the Wharton report was submitted to the SEC in 1962, underscoring the positive role that mutual funds played in capital markets. The report concluded that mutual funds provided small investors with a way to diversify the risks of investing in the stock market, thereby encouraging more widespread acceptance of the idea of investing in corporate equities. It also offered reassurance to those who worried that large fund companies would distort the movements of the markets with their buying and selling.

The biggest problems in the industry, according to the Wharton report, related to potential conflicts between the interests of shareowners and the people who managed the funds. Too often, the boards of directors of the funds were composed of the same people who owned the fund management company. The regulators wanted to make sure that the boards of directors were truly independent and represented the shareholders.

In this case, Franklin was ahead of the game, since the company had already created a board that included independent directors. By the time the SEC completed its work, Congress was generally more concerned about the over-the-counter markets. Meanwhile, the rise of the conglomerate was setting the stage for a three-year wave of horizontal mergers, beginning in 1966. This wave of mergers fed one of the strongest bull markets of the century.

THE 1960S: THE GO-GO YEARS

The 1960s, a period when America struggled through remarkable social and technological change, also demonstrated that when it came to investing, Americans were always ready to repeat history. For much of the decade, except for brief but steep market crashes in 1962, 1966 and then the big falloff during 1969–70, the market rose at a rapid pace to unprecedented levels. Competition between the United States and the U.S.S.R. to explore space, combined with the growing popularity of television and other advances in science, consumer electronics and mass communications, helped ignite a popular mania for stocks similar to the investing fever of the 1920s. Fueled by an excitable business press and a newly aggressive financial services industry, investors grew convinced that there was no end to yearly double-digit gains. Later, people would refer to this time as the go-go era.

As in many periods of rapid market growth, there was a dark side to the market boom of the 1960s. A certain amount of manipulative accounting helped fuel the prosperous times. Some start-up companies with little experience took advantage of the financial climate to issue shares and were pleased to see them sell for remarkably high multiples relative to actual earnings.

One important difference between the 1920s and 1960s was the increasingly significant role that mutual funds played in this market. By the autumn of 1965, mutual funds had become a major power in the market. Some 25 percent of the total value of stock exchange transactions resulted from trading by funds. The word on Wall Street was that "at last the funds were making 'people's capitalism' a reality instead of a catch phrase."

At the start of the decade, mutual funds retained the generally conservative image that they had developed since the postwar period. After the "little crash" of 1962, for instance, when the Dow Jones Industrial Average dropped from 735 to 535, the New York Stock Exchange issued a study that praised the fund industry for practicing a prudent investment approach that not only protected its shareholders from undue risk, but also helped keep the market stable. A new breed of more aggressive, growth-oriented mutual funds, however, came into prominence during the 1960s, following in the footsteps of the innovative Dreyfus Fund founded in the early 1950s. These so-called go-go or performance funds were characterized by a rapid turnover of holdings. Many people invested in the hottest new issues of small, untested companies that generated remarkable returns of 50 percent or more during the middle years of the decade through 1968.

As these funds became the rage, the 1960s also saw the rise of the fund manager as a media darling. One popular manager dazzled observers with his rapid-fire ability to jump in and out of stocks at seemingly just the right moment, leading to a fund turnover of 120 percent. To Charlie and Rupert, Jr., this style of "fund star" investing reinforced their natural tendency to take a team approach to investment portfolio management. Rupert often remarked that "it's the spouting whale that gets harpooned."

Many people watched in awe as the market grew in the mid-1960s. Ken Koskella was typical of hundreds of young men from the era. He had grown up in a working-class family in California and wanted to do better for his own wife and children. After putting himself through college, he landed what he thought was a good job as a salesman and marketing trainee for a large pharmaceutical company. "I ran into a guy who used to work for me," he recalls. "He was a stockbroker.... He made more money in a month than I made in a year." Convinced that he needed to change industries, Koskella signed on as a trainee with Dean Witter, but soon grew frustrated with the short-term perspective of many of his peers. In the early 1970s, Koskella left the brokerage business, eventually to join Franklin.

⁓Many others in the fund industry rejected the short-term perspective of the era, including John Templeton, who by the late 1960s believed that the market was far overvalued. Templeton sold his company in 1969 (including Templeton, Dobbrow and Vance as a subsidiary of Lexington) to Piedmont Management Company, Inc. Based in the Bahamas, far from the chaotic atmosphere and short-term investment thinking of Wall Street, Templeton continued investing, concentrating on managing his one remaining enterprise, Templeton Growth Fund, with its small contingent of loyal shareholders. As it turned out, Templeton was right to leave the market in 1969. The following year the Dow plunged nearly 35 percent.

HEADING TO CALIFORNIA

From New York, Charlie understood the importance of the California market in the 1960s. The population was booming. Late in 1962, the state surpassed New York as the most populous in the nation. Tracking the statistics from the Investment Company Institute (ICI), Charlie saw that California had become the leading market in the United States for mutual fund sales.

⁓In the 1960s, California also happened to be home to some of the leading innovators in the mutual fund industry. California was the birthplace of the financial planning industry, which added to the state's appeal. Many insurance brokers were switching industries to become financial planners and mutual fund salesmen.

⁓To tap into this booming market, in 1963 Charlie hired a wholesaler in California as a commissioned sales representative who established an independent firm called Franklin Mutual Fund Distributors. Talking to brokers, the man would ask, "What's the first bill a consumer is going to pay?" The answer was always the utilities. Talking to a group of investors, he would turn the lights off and then back on. "How would you like to make money every time someone turns on his lights in the United States?"

Franklin had 24 of the nation's best utilities in its utilities fund, which Charlie was managing. Unfortunately, Charlie's California wholesaler had a tendency to oversell. After a couple of years, Charlie realized that the man did not share his own sense of duty to the investor, and they parted company. But his legacy was important. "He showed me how you really make a story come alive," says Dick Stoker. In the meantime, Charlie searched for someone else to lead the California market.

Judson Grosvenor, a San Diego broker, first met Charlie at the annual Mutual Fund Dealers Conference in the early 1960s in Bal Harbour, Florida. Grosvenor was hard to miss. A larger-than-life character who wore bright paisley jackets in the 1960s, he was born in Ontario, Canada, and raised in Michigan. He became a stockbroker with Eastman Dillon in Southern California and was so successful with Franklin Utilities Fund that he caught Charlie's attention. When Charlie needed a new wholesaler in the region in the late 1960s, he and Grosvenor talked. By this time, Grosvenor was the resident vice president of Roberts, Scott & Company's Escondido office in Southern California. To come to Franklin was a risk,

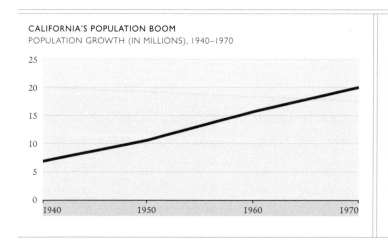

CALIFORNIA'S POPULATION BOOM
POPULATION GROWTH (IN MILLIONS), 1940–1970

Between 1940 and 1970, California's population nearly tripled, growing by almost 13 million people. This population boom created a promising market for financial planners and mutual funds.

To promote the use of Keogh retirement plans in the mid-1960s, Franklin's Dick Stoker used a fictional newspaper in presentations to brokers and financial planners. He transformed the Keogh acronym to "Keep Earnings Out of Govt. Hands."

JUDSON GROSVENOR

He wore a white suit and a Panama hat and often came bearing gifts. When Judson Grosvenor arrived at Franklin's tiny offices on Wall Street in the 1960s, he brought a bag full of California oranges. He was loud and friendly with everyone.

"He created this plastic accordion folder," says Rupert, Jr., "which he spread out on the table when he called on brokers." The folder contained copies of big orders—25,000 from one person, 100,000 from another. "'Look what other people are doing with this fund,' he would say. 'Look at the commissions you can earn with Franklin.'"

but Grosvenor believed in the product. In January 1969 he made the move. It was an auspicious moment; share prices on the New York Stock Exchange were at an all-time high.

SENSIBLE SPECULATION THROUGH DYNATECH

With the market steaming forward in 1968, Franklin had launched a new fund, called Franklin DynaTech. Charlie created and managed this fund to satisfy investor demand for growth at the height of the go-go era. DynaTech offered a mix of stocks, which was characterized as "sensible speculation." The fund invested in hot technology sectors like computers, as well as growth industries like convalescent homes, oceanography and pollution control. It also picked up undervalued equities known as special situations.

DynaTech also held a significant portion of its assets in South African gold stocks. The gold stocks were a drag on performance in 1968, but they offered "a hedge against what politicians might do." The fixed price of gold was under heavy pressure. Starting in 1968, central banks around the world had moved to end their efforts to maintain the price of gold at the official exchange rate of $35 per ounce. The breakdown of the old monetary order, combined with the expense and anxiety produced by the Vietnam War, rising interest rates in the United States and rising inflation worldwide, sparked a rush by investors to gold. The production of gold did not increase during this period. Thus, a readjustment in gold's value was likely. When that happened, gold was expected to appreciate significantly.

⌁DynaTech's position in gold reflected Franklin's continuing conservatism, even at the height of the go-go market, and a cautious attitude in other aspects of DynaTech's portfolio. The fund did not invest in the hot franchise restaurant industry, for example, because by the time DynaTech was launched "the franchise story was pretty well known on Wall Street," Charlie told a reporter. Instead, DynaTech looked for emerging industries like convalescent homes. When a company called Extendicare went public in this sector in February 1968, its share price soared from the offering of $8 to $19. DynaTech accumulated shares as

CHARLES B. JOHNSON, PRESIDENT, FRANKLIN DISTRIBUTORS
See Page 5

Persistence brought Franklin into the limelight. In May 1969, Charlie Johnson was featured on the cover of *The Stock Market Magazine*. The article highlighted Franklin's diversified product line, with Charlie touting investors' ability to convert from one fund to another free of charge.

the price trended down over the next six months. By January 1969, the stock was trading around $68 on a split-adjusted basis.

In its first 12 months of operation, DynaTech recorded a 49.2 percent increase per share and was ranked among the top 10 performers in the industry. Net assets grew from $2 million in March 1968 to more than $11 million in less than a year.

Overall, the 1960s were very good to the mutual fund industry. Between 1959 and 1969, mutual funds grew 206 percent as assets under management rose from $15.8 billion to $48.3 billion. This growth rate exceeded that of savings and loans, commercial banks, mutual savings banks and life insurance companies, though relative to these other major players, the fund industry was still a minor player.

END OF THE GO-GO ERA

It was inevitable that the overheated markets of the 1960s would cool off, and they did. After the Dow Jones Industrial Average reached highs of close to 1,000 during 1966 and 1968, the market finally collapsed in late 1969 and 1970. By May 1970, the Dow was at 631, and the total value of all stocks on the New York Stock Exchange was half what it had been at the beginning of 1969. Worse, many of the market favorites of the time, including computer and electronics companies and franchisers, were down 80 percent to 90 percent.

In 1971 David Babson, an old-guard investment counselor since the early 1930s, was asked, "What happened?" In response, he echoed the views of many when he lamented the general loss of a sense of responsibility among "the professionals" on the Street. Among his litany of faults, Babson included too many accountants who "played footsie" with stock-promoting managements and had too much faith in the "conglomerate movement." He also faulted too many investment advisors "who massacred clients' portfolios" while trying to "make good on the over-promises that they had made to attract the business in the first place." Finally, he blamed "security analysts who forgot about their professional ethics to become 'story peddlers' and who let their institutions get taken in by a whole parade of confidence men."

Yet for many investing professionals and their shareholders, the 1960s were not such a turbulent decade after all. As Babson noted, "For those who stuck to their guns, who tried to follow a progressive but realistic approach, who didn't prostitute their professional responsibilities, who didn't get seduced by conflicts of interest, who didn't get suckered into glib 'concepts,' nothing much really did go wrong." In many ways, Babson was describing Franklin. Rather than get drawn into the euphoria of the era, Franklin had stayed focused on building the organization and selling investors on the importance of diversity and a long-term strategy.

Consumer disenchantment with the industry followed the market downturn, and Congress soon took steps to change the rules in the mutual fund industry. In 1970 it passed the Investment Company Amendments Act, which imposed stricter fiduciary standards on the managers, officers and directors of investment companies. The Act also made it easier for shareholders to challenge fund management fees. Overall, the new rules sought to strengthen and protect the rights of shareholders.

Franklin adjusted to the downturn in the equities markets by introducing Franklin U.S. Government Securities Fund, which was designed to provide investors with current income. Franklin offered investors the

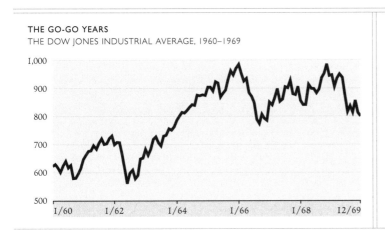

THE GO-GO YEARS
THE DOW JONES INDUSTRIAL AVERAGE, 1960–1969

From its bottom in 1962 (the mini-crash), the Dow Jones Industrial Average rose dramatically through the end of 1965. The market then slumped, but rebounded to nearly match its previous high by the middle of 1969.

ability to move their money between the Franklin funds. This would allow them to rebalance their portfolio to maintain proper diversification when markets turned around. The new fund gave Franklin an important marketing tool. In an overheated market, investors could move their assets to the sidelines without leaving Franklin's family. With inflation running high and interest rates rising, government securities also offered attractive yields. With this new fund, Franklin hoped to find a way to continue to grow, but the Johnsons faced the entrepreneur's classic dilemma.

Throughout the 1960s, Charlie had looked for ways to sustain the growth of Franklin and to realize some of the value that had been created. At one point in the mid-1960s, Delphi Management, a business owned by members of the du Pont family, offered to buy Franklin in an all-stock deal. Charlie turned them down. Instead, he moved ahead with his own

A new income fund 1970

Franklin Introduces U.S. Securities Fund

Franklin Custodian Funds, Inc., New York, announced the introduction of a new mutual fund, the Franklin U.S. Government Securities Fund. The new entry will limit its investments to securities which are obligations of the U.S. Government or its instrumentalities. (An instrumentality is a government agency organized under federal charter with government supervision).

The investment objective of the new fund, according to Charles B. Johnson, a director, and president of Franklin Distributors Inc., the management company, is to obtain current income. The initial offering price per share will be $10 plus

CHARLES B. JOHNSON

the basic sales charge. Thereafter shares will be offered at a price computed on net asset value plus a standard sales charge.

A unique feature of the fund, exclusive with Frank- (Continued on Page 16)

plan. Late in 1969, Franklin Resources, Inc., was incorporated in Delaware as a holding company with Franklin Distributors as a subsidiary. This was the first step along the path to going public.

GOING PUBLIC

Taking Franklin public was not an easy task. As a holding company, Franklin Resources owned a broker/dealer. The NASD had placed a number of restrictions on broker/dealers who hoped to go public, and some in the industry feared that the government might close the door completely. Stalled by the SEC over these issues, Charlie called Bill Lippman. Lippman had left King Merritt to launch his own brokerage firm, William Jennings & Co. In 1964 he created Pilgrim Fund, a mutual fund focused on financial services. Five years later, with the help of an attorney named Murray Simpson, he took his company public. Lippman suggested that Charlie contact Simpson.

A Chicago native, Simpson had worked for the SEC in the early 1960s before joining the Philadelphia law firm of Stradley Ronon Stevens and Young. By 1970 Simpson had moved back to Chicago and launched his own law firm. With Simpson's legal help and expertise, Franklin was able to win SEC approval, and the company went public in May 1971. A month later, Simpson joined the board of directors and became outside counsel to the company.

Franklin's initial public offering of 120,000 shares at $5 a share raised $600,000. The shares traded in the over-the-counter market. With this cash in hand, Charlie and Rupert, Jr., believed they were well positioned for the future. But it was still a small operation. At 99 Wall Street, visitors rode a rickety elevator to the 22nd floor, one floor short of the top. In this office, Charlie, Rupert, Jerry Palmieri, Sam Morse and a handful of others worked with their shirtsleeves rolled up.

Optimistic about Franklin's future, broker Harold Jacob created this cartoon. He then sent it to Charlie and Rupert, Jr., with best wishes.

Chapter II

The
Hard Years

Mutual fund industry veteran Henry Lou Jamieson was at a crossroads after his high-flying firm, Winfield and Co., stumbled at the end of the 1960s' go-go years. In 1971 his conversation with Charlie Johnson at an industry convention would have a far-reaching impact on the future of both companies.

Opposite: The Golden State's most enduring symbol.

The
Hard Years

*Industry, perseverance and frugality
make fortune yield.*

— BENJAMIN FRANKLIN

Winfield Growth
Fund logo
1970

When the mutual fund industry gathered for its annual convention in Washington, D.C., in 1971, a number of companies were reeling from the collapse of the bull market. Each of the companies at the convention had a sales booth. Brokers came to be wined and dined and learn about the individual funds. It was also a chance to scout opportunities.

It was at this convention that Bill Lippman introduced Charlie to Henry Lou Jamieson, the president of Winfield and Co., a California-based mutual fund manager. Jamieson was an industry veteran who sold his first mutual fund in 1940. In 1967 Jamieson's daughter had married Bob Hagopian, a securities salesman who teamed up with David Meid, a 31-year-old portfolio manager, to purchase a significant share of Winfield and Co. Hagopian asked Jamieson to move to California and become president of Winfield.

Organized in Kansas in 1959, Winfield and Co. had been a fairly undistinguished mutual fund manager prior to 1965. After the new team took over, assets under management in the renamed Winfield Growth Fund (formerly Winfield Growth Industries Fund) skyrocketed from $11 million in 1965 to $205 million in 1967. Featured in a book called *The New Breed on Wall Street*, Meid seemed to represent the attitude of the times. In 1968 he confessed to a reporter, "I never read research reports anymore." He described himself as "a merchandise manager in a department store. I look for what's going to sell next year."

When the market collapsed, Winfield ran into trouble. Winfield Growth Fund lost 37 percent in the year ended September 30, 1970, one of the biggest losers in the mutual fund industry. The SEC launched an investigation, and both Hagopian and Meid withdrew from active management. Working to restructure the company's operations and improve its relationship with regulators, Jamieson hired Harmon Burns, a young regulator who had recently left the SEC. Quietly and cautiously, Jamieson also began looking for an angel to acquire the business.

Charlie Johnson was interested in Winfield despite its problems. The company had three good funds: Winfield Growth Fund, WinCap Fund and its AGE Fund, which was sold only to members of the Assembly of Government Employees. The company also had its own transfer agency, Applied Financial Systems (AFS), which was 60 percent owned by Winfield and operated out of the same building at 155 Bovet Road in San Mateo. AFS had worked with IBM's Service Bureau Corporation to develop one of the best transfer agent systems in the mutual fund industry. Frustrated by the service they were getting from the Bank of New York, which was their transfer agent at the time, Charlie and Rupert, Jr., hoped that by owning the transfer agency, they could improve the quality of customer service. Acquiring Winfield, a company with more than twice Franklin's net assets under management, would also move Franklin to a new level and greater efficiencies. Charlie was also attracted by Winfield's presence in the California market, which was growing, and on the cutting edge of innovation in the industry.

As they talked, Jamieson and Johnson liked each other. Jamieson felt that Franklin offered prudent and stable management. Winfield was in a difficult situation. The ownership of the company was divided among three groups, none of which held a majority position. One group included Jamieson and a number of current employees. Another group included ex-employees, led by David Meid. Meid had left the company, but still owned a significant stake. At the same time, Farmers Insurance Company, having recognized that Winfield was in trouble and spotting an opportunity to develop a foothold in the mutual fund business, had purchased Winfield shares from several other partners. Tensions between these three groups were high. Farmers Insurance had filed a lawsuit against the current management group.

Franklin was in a good position to acquire Winfield, despite Winfield's larger size. With a publicly traded stock, Franklin had the ability to finance the deal and to offer stock to the existing owners. Nevertheless, there were risks. To some people, Winfield looked like a sinking ship. Franklin might get sucked under by the acquisition, especially given the rapidly deteriorating situation in the market.

After his conversation with Jamieson, Charlie moved to diffuse the fight between the shareholders. He made a deal with Meid and then began acquiring Winfield stock in August 1972. Putting all the pieces of the deal together wasn't easy. To satisfy one group of shareholders, he agreed that the transfer agency would be spun off as a stand-alone business, hoping that close business ties would still improve Franklin's service operations. To finance the acquisition of Winfield, Franklin sold 3,000 shares of $6.50 convertible preferred stock to raise $225,000. The company also obtained a loan from the Small Business Administration. Raising this money gave Franklin the financial wherewithal to acquire Winfield after finalizing separate purchase transactions with each of the three shareholder groups and satisfying pending regulatory issues. By the time the deal was completed in January 1973, the combined organization had close to $250 million in assets under management.

Integrating Winfield posed major challenges for Franklin. Should the company shrink Winfield's operation in California, handling shareholder services operations there while maintaining headquarters in New York? Or should it downsize on Wall Street and relocate the headquarters to San Mateo? Jamieson had hoped that Charlie would decide to move to California, and he lowered the purchase price to secure this commitment. Had it been some other part of the country, Charlie says, they might have made a different decision, "but San Francisco was an attractive area." The Johnsons were also influenced by the fact that more than half of the company's business was being done in California. Charlie and Rupert decided they would give it a try. "If it doesn't work, we can always move back," Charlie thought.

The move posed challenges to the Johnson household. While taking care of a family that had now grown to seven children, Ann had gone back to school to finish her degree. After graduating from Seton Hall, she had enrolled at the New Jersey Medical School, beginning her courses around the time that Charlie completed the Winfield deal. Not wanting to take the children out of school or disrupt Ann's medical education, Charlie rented an apartment in San Mateo and commuted to the West Coast from January to July 1973. In the spring of 1973, the Johnsons bought a house in the nearby community of Hillsborough. The house had once belonged to a Winfield executive, but many of the rooms had never been finished. Charlie bought the house in an auction, and over the summer, he had a crew get it ready. At the end of the summer, Charlie's family moved west. The children enrolled in school, and Ann continued her medical education at Stanford University.

Rupert, Jr., remained in New York for several months to supervise operations. The Franklin staff of nearly 30 employees was reduced substantially and relocated to the Lincoln Building on 43rd Street and Fifth Avenue in Manhattan. Jerry Palmieri stayed behind to manage Franklin Growth Fund and maintain a presence for Franklin in New York. By the time Rupert joined Charlie in California, the combined staff of the two organizations had been reduced by 15 to 20 people, or roughly 25 percent. Charlie and Rupert hoped these efficiencies would make the organization more profitable.

～Weeks after the Winfield acquisition was completed, *Barron's* featured Charlie and Franklin funds in an article—a rare media moment for a company that was still only a small player in the mutual fund industry. The article noted that the combined company had about $230 million in assets under management, out of a total of $58 billion invested in the mutual fund industry. Nevertheless, it seemed poised for growth.

REORGANIZING THE COMBINED COMPANY

After arriving in California, Charlie had to gauge the strengths and weaknesses of the people in the Winfield organization and reconcile various competing visions for the future. Jamieson, for example, was clearly an outstanding salesman. "My father loved wholesaling," recalls his son, Ed Jamieson, "and I don't think he particularly liked managing a firm." Under the new structure, Lou Jamieson became chairman of Franklin Distributors in January 1973. Charlie served as chief executive officer and chairman of Franklin Resources.

～Jamieson also had ideas about how the company should grow. He had frequently suggested to potential Winfield acquirers that the company was ready to launch a dual distribution system working through broker/dealers and "a national captive sales organization." Charlie did not want to jeopardize his relationships in the broker/dealer community by moving into direct sales to investors, but he was willing to expand the wholesale effort.

～Another Winfield employee who made an immediately good impression on Charlie was Harmon Burns. The two got to know each other on a drive to Lake Tahoe for a big meeting of the Assembly of Government Employees. "I drove my dad's car," Burns remembers.

～"We had a chance to talk," says Charlie, "and it came across very clearly to me that Burns was a very solid citizen with good judgment.

In 1974 the board and officers of Research Equity
Fund (formerly Winfield Growth Fund) helped
build regulatory and investor confidence in the
fund's operations. Seated (L-R): Frank Adams, David
Garbellano, Martin Wiskemann, Henry Lou Jamieson,
Philip Russell. Standing (L-R): Frank "Budd"
Abbott, Charlie Johnson, Harold Pepperall, Frank
LaHaye, Harmon Burns, Rupert H. Johnson, Jr.

HENRY LOU JAMIESON

Henry Lou Jamieson's mother sold mutual funds in the 1920s. Growing up in Fort Wayne, Indiana, "Lou," also known as "Jamie" among his friends, came of age during the Depression. He graduated from George Washington University and then followed in his mother's footsteps to the mutual fund industry. During World War II, he served in the navy in San Francisco. He remained in the Bay Area after the war and eventually launched his own financial planning firm.

An outstanding salesman with tremendous energy and knowledge, Jamieson did well. King Merritt, the leader of a very successful mutual fund sales organization, recognized his abilities and recruited him to New York to manage his famous brokerage, but Jamieson didn't stay on the East Coast. When his daughter married Bob Hagopian, Jamieson agreed to return to San Francisco to manage his new son-in-law's mutual fund company—Winfield. After Franklin's acquisition of Winfield, Jamieson served as a mentor to many people in the sales organization.

I developed a lot of confidence in him just from three or four hours driving with him."

Charlie, Rupert and Sam Morse also discovered that they had much in common with other members of the senior management team at Winfield, including R. Martin Wiskemann and wholesaler Earl Johnson (no relation to Charlie and Rupert). The Swiss-born Wiskemann was an outstanding portfolio manager. Johnson, a Korean War-era veteran, worked in Southern California as a wholesaler.

For their part, the team at Winfield was pleased to have a new perspective after the company's previous difficulties with the government. "I was happy to get some new, younger blood on the management team," Burns remembers, "especially from the financial establishment back East." Sam Morse, who had supervised Franklin's operations, mentored Burns. Wiskemann, a portfolio manager who owned a significant number of shares in Winfield, became the third-largest shareholder of Franklin after the acquisition. Many Winfield employees were also pleased with the deal. They had feared that Farmers Insurance would take Winfield's assets and integrate operations with their existing business in Southern California. With the Franklin team, they had the opportunity to continue to shape their own destiny.

Around this same time, Franklin moved Jud Grosvenor north to become national sales manager. Grosvenor began recruiting other salespeople, but with tight budgets, hiring was a challenge. Tom Cotter, Franklin's 25th employee, took over sales for northern California and the Pacific Northwest just prior to the Winfield acquisition. After the merger and the company's move to California, Cotter developed an appreciation for Rupert, Jr., and Charlie. "They were easygoing guys. It was a tough market in which to work. They didn't set quotas. As long as we were showing the flag and trying to do a good job, they were behind us."

THE MARKET HITS BOTTOM

As the long-running bull market reversed direction in 1970, the financial press reported the decline with grim regularity. The growing enthusiasm of many middle-class investors for equity mutual funds was suddenly lost. Yearly redemptions exceeded sales in equity funds throughout the 1970s.

For about 18 months leading up to January 1973, stocks did make a strong if short-lived recovery, and the Dow Jones Industrial Average finally passed the 1,000 mark in November 1972. However, a disheartening market collapse soon followed in the face of continuing negative political and economic news, including Watergate and the discredited Nixon administration, the United States' continued involvement in a losing and costly war with Vietnam, the OPEC oil embargo and continuing inflation.

At the bottom of the market, the ICI held its annual convention in Williamsburg, Virginia. "Usually the meeting was in Hawaii or in some fancy resort," Charlie remembers, "but that year they had it in Williamsburg" so that people could drive and save the cost of airfare. "It rained, and it was just miserable, and everybody was down in the dumps."

In bad times on Wall Street, some of the most successful investors were those who fished in dangerous waters. In New York, an investor named Max Heine focused on what people called special situations, companies whose values were shifting quickly because of takeover bids or asset liquidations, including bankruptcies. His Mutual Shares Corp.

was one of roughly 150 fund companies to outpace the bull market rallies of the Dow in 1975 and 1976. The assets in the fund actually appreciated during the severe bear market of 1974. While the average mutual fund fell 21 percent in this three-year period, Mutual Shares gained 34 percent. Mutual Shares' success, however, was uncharacteristic of the industry.

⮰As equity mutual fund redemption rates reached alarming levels, some observers began wondering if the industry was due to disappear altogether. Ironically, what helped save the industry was the same thing that was rattling the stock market: worsening inflation and rising interest rates ("stagflation"). As people grew nervous about the market and moved their money back to the safety of federally insured bank accounts, they found, to their growing dismay, that inflation was making banks a far less attractive alternative than they had hoped. While inflation seemed to have no limit, the savings account rates offered by banks were fixed by the federal government at 4.5 percent. Unable to earn a decent rate of return on their savings accounts, investors grew increasingly anxious about their financial futures. Under pressure from the bear market, Charlie and Rupert looked for ways to meet the needs of these investors.

FRANKLIN RESPONDS TO THE MARKET DOWNTURN
Franklin's response to the financial doldrums of the 1970s was to act quickly to find creative ways to provide investors with new investment opportunities. In 1973 with investor approval, Franklin took Research Capital Fund—the ailing former WinCap Fund, which was down around 50 percent from its 1969 highs—and changed its focus to gold-mining and natural resources stocks. For the sales force, the gold fund proved to be a hit. "One time I was in a brokerage office," recalled Tom Cotter, "and the manager said, 'None of the representatives will sit still for a [mutual fund] wholesaler.' But he was interested in gold ownership. I got halfway through my presentation and a guy pointed his finger at me and said, 'He's a mutual fund wholesaler.' But by then they were interested enough in the gold story that they stuck it out."

As one of the first funds oriented toward gold stocks, Research Capital was an immediate hit with investors. Assets under management more than tripled from $8 million to $25 million within six months of the switch. This success was partly a result of perfect timing. Gold stocks surged in the first half of the 1970s in reaction to inflation and the U.S. decision to abandon the $35 an ounce peg. Such enthusiasm for gold investing had not been seen since the 1930s. Charlie also worked hard to promote the fund. In April of 1974, investors and their families were invited (for a registration fee of $45) to attend an all-day "San Francisco Gold Symposium" sponsored by Franklin Resources. The event featured the editor of a mining journal from the United Kingdom and other "international experts" discussing opportunities in gold investing, along with Martin Wiskemann and Charlie Johnson from Franklin.

Martin Wiskemann

The gold fund was undeniably risky, and Lou Jamieson, who was president of the fund, warned investors in a short interview in *The New York Times* that the rush to gold could push prices to unwarranted heights. For investors who lacked faith in the value of the dollar during this difficult economic period, the gold fund even announced a program that provided shareholders the option of receiving dividends in the reassuring form of gold coins, including the "Austrian 100-corona, South African kruggerand and Mexican 20-peso." Gold funds did indeed fall to earth in 1975 and 1976 as gold prices tumbled, but in 1977 Research Capital Fund was the top-performing fund in the United States, with a gain of 44.3 percent over the previous year.

The gold fund saved the company for about two years. According to a longtime employee, the gold fund "started to right the ship." It brought new investors to Franklin. Franklin then launched a new service that made it easy for them to move into other investments for a nominal fee. To hold onto these new investors, Franklin developed new income and bond funds. Bonds, an especially difficult investment for the small investor to manage, became an ideal way for Franklin to attract shareholders who were wary of stocks and frustrated by low bank rates.

NEW VENTURES

As the market softened in the early 1970s, Charlie and Rupert struggled to find new ways to meet investor needs. Even before the deal with Winfield, they explored a proposal by Jud Grosvenor and his son, Mark, to develop land in Southern California. Franklin formed two subsidiaries in 1971: Jaymark Financial, Inc., and Cramar Investments, Inc. Jaymark focused on the development of real estate investments, purchasing tracts of raw land. Cramar concentrated on retail land sales. Unfortunately, the venture into real estate did not go well. "It didn't turn out to be as easy a business as it was made out to be," says Charlie. Rather than put additional capital into the enterprise, Franklin sold Jaymark in February 1973.

Franklin also acquired a financial planning company called Financial Service Corp., and started Franklin Energy Corp. to invest in the oil and gas industry.

In 1978 Charlie brought in John Dolan and Ken Koskella to establish Franklin Asset Management, as an investment advisor. Both Dolan and Koskella had previously run their own firms. Each brought a modest number of clients to Franklin. Franklin provided some marketing support, and they went to work to build the business.

Overall, Franklin's efforts to diversify in the 1970s reflected an ongoing effort to help investors under various market conditions. "Charlie was interested in experimenting in ways that would give leverage to our core business, but only if it helped our mutual fund business," says Dick Stoker. Like many entrepreneurial firms, the company tested the boundaries of its organizational capabilities. Despite some successes, Charlie and Rupert found that their greatest strengths lay in their traditional area of expertise in the mutual fund business. But staying afloat until the market turned back in Franklin's direction was not easy.

During these years, Franklin struggled financially. When assets under management declined to $166 million in 1977, the company generated little or no cash flow. Salaries were frozen. The executives took pay cuts. Charlie reviewed every bill, paying the most urgent and deferring those that could be put off a little longer. Wearing his green eyeshade, Sam Morse made sure the office supplies were carefully rationed.

Earl Johnson remembers, "We were saving paper clips from mail that people sent to us, sharpening small pencils and cutting envelopes we received to make scratch paper." Johnson, who had joined Winfield in 1967, found that by the mid-1970s he couldn't make enough money to support his wife and three children. Over lunch one day in 1976, he told Charlie and Jamieson that he had decided to take a marketing job with a large Southern California real estate company. "It was the hardest thing I ever had to do," Earl Johnson recalls.

Some people who had invested in Franklin stock decided it was time to sell. Since the IPO in 1971, the price had fallen from $5 to less than $1 a share—if the stock traded at all. Few broker/dealers handled the stock. For those who wanted to sell, however, Charlie and Rupert, Jr., found buyers. Jud and Mark Grosvenor bought shares as they became available. Lou Jamieson decided to sell out in this era, but he had a different reason. Struggling with health problems in the late 1970s, Jamieson told Charlie he would like to leave his position at Franklin Resources to become an independent director on the fund boards. To do so, according to SEC rules, he would have to sell his shares in Franklin Resources. Charlie honored Jamieson's request, and Jamieson became chairman of the various fund boards. Years later, his son, Ed, recalls a conversation that he and his father had while on vacation. "We were in a rowboat at a resort in the Poconos. He said, 'Do you know what my shares would have been worth today?' When he told me, I almost fell out of the boat."

While the company was still small, communication among Franklin's employees was easy. Charlie's door was open. The mantra for the company's 34 full-time employees in 1977 reflected the advice of Benjamin Franklin: "Don't waste money, don't spend money you don't have." Employees understood that cost-saving measures weren't done just to save money, they were an absolute necessity. "I was looking at the business to make sure that we were going to survive," says Charlie.

Throughout these lean years, Franklin emphasized service. "You try to figure out a way to differentiate yourself in the mutual fund industry," Harmon Burns recalls, "and there aren't that many ways. It's so easy to copy a fund.... We thought the one thing we might be able to do to set us apart would be service to the shareholders and the brokers. That was one of the guiding features of the business plan." Unfortunately, the anticipated advantages of the close relationship with Applied Financial Systems, Franklin's transfer agency, were often hard to achieve.

As Franklin struggled to take care of the day-to-day needs of the business, Charlie encouraged everyone to stay focused. He rarely gave speeches to employees. He led by example. He worked hard. He didn't complain. The company prided itself on its frugality. "It was really the strength of Charlie's will that got the company through that period," says Burns.

COMPETITION UNLEASHED BY REGULATORY REFORM

By the mid-1970s, confidence in government had begun to wane. A new generation of economists had begun to persuasively argue for deregulation. Policymakers at the SEC listened. In 1975 they lifted the rules that fixed brokerage fees for stock trades. Immediately, a host of discount brokers began to challenge the operations of well-established Wall Street firms like Merrill Lynch. With these new firms, self-directed investors could increasingly bypass the traditional broker/dealer networks to place their own trades with minimal transaction costs. At first, these new discount brokers were dismissed by many people in the securities industry, but they signaled the beginning of a phenomenon that would eventually reshape the world of investing.

As part of its effort to stimulate greater competition in the securities industry, the SEC also began to relax the rules on advertising. In the mutual fund industry, companies were finally allowed to do more than simply mention the fund's name and investment objectives. By opening the business to greater competitive pressures, the SEC helped launch a new era in the mutual fund industry.

The movement by some fund companies to sell directly to investors also fueled the rise of the no-load mutual fund. Franklin resisted this trend. As Charlie told a *Barron's* reporter in 1973, "I think the future belongs to the full-load industry. Mutual funds are still sold, not bought, and a person is not going to buy unless a salesman is out there explaining the business, giving him reasons for investing in the funds." No-loads, Charlie said, might work for sophisticated investors, but not for the average person.

Charlie also spoke out against the idea of negotiated commissions on mutual funds. Three things would happen if commissions were set by competition, he argued: Brokerage houses would stop selling open-end mutual funds, closed-end fund underwritings would soar, and existing open-end funds would be forced to set up their own retail sales organizations. He continued to believe in the value of professional advice and the role of brokers as investor advisors.

(L-R): Rupert H. Johnson, Jr., Martin Wiskemann, John Chapin, Jud Grosvenor, Earl Johnson and Tom Cotter gathered for a financial planning convention in the mid-1970s.

New federal laws soon brought more investors in the door. The investment industry received a boost on Labor Day in 1974 when President Gerald Ford signed the Employee Retirement Income Security Act (ERISA). The new law created the Individual Retirement Account (IRA) and allowed wage earners not covered by a retirement plan to set money aside in a tax-deferred account. Many hailed the new accounts as a promising marketing opportunity for mutual funds, in part because the rules precluded the investor from changing where the money was invested more frequently than once every three years.

But the volatility of the early 1970s stock and bond markets made many investors reluctant to lock into a single type of investment vehicle for that length of time. Franklin was quick to advertise a solution to this problem. In 1974 Franklin became one of the first fund companies to allow investors to move assets between funds for a nominal fee with just a phone call. In an industry that commonly required a great deal of paperwork to make adjustments in fund investments, this innovation was attractive to investors. Speaking to *Newsweek* in 1975, Lou Jamieson highlighted how this telephone switching feature was especially valuable for investors who set up their IRA with a fund company like Franklin that offered a diverse array of funds. Now, he said, "the IRA customer can switch from one fund to another with no tax consequences and no commissions." That year, *BusinessWeek* also praised Franklin for the flexibility it offered an IRA investor:

> . . . because its seven funds present a wide spectrum. One is a gold fund, one is solely in utilities, and one buys discount bonds. One sticks to high-quality growth stocks, one seeks capital gains in natural resource shares, and one is devoted to government securities—a kind of cash haven when all other plays look bleak. Yet another invests in small companies whose shares might rocket in speculative periods.

The only fee investors incurred at Franklin for moving between funds was a maximum $5 fee for each transaction. Franklin thus positioned itself as an optimal choice for investors looking for the ability to diversify their assets within one company while maintaining flexibility.

Despite the initial enthusiasm about the opportunities IRAs opened for the mutual fund industry, it became apparent within a few years that many predictions were overly optimistic. The number of new IRAs certainly exceeded some expectations, reaching 2.5 million accounts holding a total of $2.6 billion by the end of 1977, but only a small percentage of these accounts were held in mutual funds. Most people put their money in savings accounts, life insurance annuities or Treasury bonds. The old Keogh plans, which had been around since 1964 but were simplified under ERISA, were far more successful for the fund industry, which managed 42 percent of these types of accounts. Like the gold fund, the IRA attracted some investors, but it was hardly a cure-all for the things that were ailing Franklin.

CASH FLOW ISSUES

Throughout the 1970s, Franklin struggled to turn a profit. Relocation expenses associated with the Winfield acquisition and the move to California, combined with the shutdown of the Southern California real estate venture, led to a loss of nearly $118,000 in 1973. The following year, Franklin also lost money, but just barely, reporting a net loss of approximately $3,000.

Without money for advertising, the company had to sell its funds through commissioned salesmen, who were compensated largely through the fees and commissions their sales generated. By the end of the fiscal year in 1977, Franklin had just under $167 million in assets under management. By comparison, a number of other firms that had been established in the late 1940s—including T. Rowe Price, Dreyfus and Fidelity—had more than $1 billion in assets under management and could afford large sales staffs and incentives.

In response to the crisis in the industry, some mutual fund companies changed their strategies. Fidelity and Wellington eliminated front-end sales charges. Franklin's management discussed this option. "The salespeople were adamantly against it," remembers Burns. "I think that as an organization we had faith that the market would come back." As a team they also believed in the value of the advice that brokers provided to investors.

⟋At Franklin, Lou Jamieson strove to keep people motivated. "He was a mentor," remembers Koskella, "the salesman's salesman." Charlie rarely showed evidence of the stress he was under. He never suggested that Ann withdraw from Stanford Medical School, despite the cost of the tuition. "He didn't come home and talk about the problems. I learned a lot of things by hearing him talk to somebody else," Ann remembers. A neighbor who lived across the street was also in the mutual fund business. Ann remembers the neighbor suffered from migraines that he attributed to the stress of those hard years. "He told me once, 'I look at Charlie. He never seems stressed. He always seems very relaxed. How does he do it?'" On the rare occasions when Charlie did evidence the stress he was under, people were surprised. One night, home during his college years, Charlie's son Chuck left a light on downstairs as he headed to bed. His father angrily told him to turn it off. "I thought, what's the big deal?" Chuck remembers. In retrospect he realized it was just one sign of the stress his father was feeling.

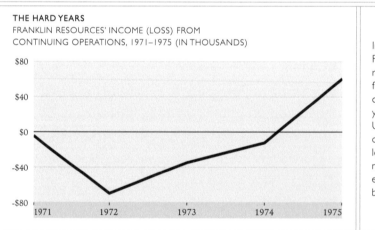

THE HARD YEARS
FRANKLIN RESOURCES' INCOME (LOSS) FROM
CONTINUING OPERATIONS, 1971–1975 (IN THOUSANDS)

$80				
$40				
$0				
-$40				
-$80				
1971	1972	1973	1974	1975

In the early 1970s, Franklin Resources recorded a loss from continuing operations four years in a row. Under the pressure of these sustained losses, Franklin's management cut expenses to the bone to survive.

While Charlie Johnson looks on, wholesaler Tom Cotter greets a guest at the Franklin booth at the 1977 International Association of Financial Planners convention in Los Angeles. Franklin saw the potential for financial planners to become a major force in the investment business.

In acquiring Winfield, Franklin had focused on benefits that included doubling the asset base, acquiring Winfield's transfer agency and securing a stronger presence in the California market. Through the 1970s, the pay-off from these aspects of the acquisition proved elusive.

The challenges arose soon after Franklin moved to California. Very little data could be moved electronically from the Bank of New York transfer agent system to Applied Financial Systems (AFS), the transfer agency that had been spun off as part of the Winfield acquisition. "We had to essentially start with the customer's name, the broker and the current balance," says Frank Isola, who worked for AFS at the time. "If a Franklin customer had a question about transactions in an account, you had to go to file boxes, which were in account number order and contained slips of paper ('fanfolds'), each of which detailed the individual transactions occurring in a customer's account."

Charlie Johnson in his office at 155 Bovet Road in San Mateo. The downturn of the mid-1970s spread gloom throughout the mutual fund industry, but according to co-workers and family members, Charlie rarely showed stress during this difficult period.

With only a flight of stairs to travel at 155 Bovet Road, Charlie and Rupert frequently visited AFS CEO Dick Lucas to express dismay at the pace and the difficulty of the conversion. Lucas had been a longtime employee at IBM and was head of IBM's Service Bureau for the entire West Coast when he began working with Winfield in the early 1970s to develop a state-of-the-art transfer agency operation that involved 100,000 customer accounts. With Franklin's acquisition of Winfield, AFS had been spun off as an independent company with Lucas as CEO. Relationships frayed. On one occasion, Charlie announced that he intended to terminate the relationship. "I remember he got so mad," says Burns, but Charlie kept his control. Stunned, AFS revamped its procedures. It was a symbiotic relationship; neither company could survive without the other at that moment, and neither had capital to spare.

At the time of the acquisition, Charlie and Rupert also believed that Winfield had cleaned up its pre-acquisition legal and regulatory problems. But at the end of the 1970s, a federal court entered a $1.2 million verdict against Winfield and Co., Inc. (WinCo). Franklin appealed. The company's lawyers felt they could win the appeal on the merits, but if they lost, they believed Franklin was entitled to indemnification under an insurance policy that WinCo had purchased. For the industry as a whole, this was an important case. Mutual funds relied on these so-called "broker's blanket bonds" to protect themselves from fraud. Initially, both the ICI and the SEC filed briefs to support Franklin's case. But after the Ninth Circuit Court of Appeals ruled against Winfield, the U.S. Supreme Court refused to hear the case. When the insurance carrier refused to cover the award, "it really blindsided us," says Charlie. Suddenly, Franklin had to make a major cash payment from its capital.

Franklin was able to take this major challenge and turn it into an opportunity. In negotiations with the plaintiffs in the case, the company agreed to infuse $200,000 into the still-existing corporate entity of Winfield and Co. and then abandon that business to the creditors. Since the acquisition value of Winfield had been so much higher, Franklin was able to take a major tax write-off. This was at a time when Franklin was just beginning to show good earnings, thanks to a new product that would revolutionize the industry.

MONEY FUNDS OFFER AN OPPORTUNITY

Many stockbrokers in the United States left the profession at the bottom of the market in 1974. Charlie's brother Andrew Johnson was among them. After 20 years on Wall Street, he sold his interest in his firm and sat down to talk with Charlie and Rupert. With his experiences in the brokerage business and as a marketer, Andy felt he could help Charlie and Rupert increase the company's assets.

Andy's arrival at Franklin coincided with conversations that Charlie and Rupert were having about launching a money fund. Money market funds had originated on the East Coast. Henry B. R. Brown and Bruce R. Bent, founders of Reserve Fund, had studied the Investment Company Act of 1940 and realized that a specially designed mutual fund could provide an elegant and lawful method to get around the Federal Reserve Board's Regulation Q, which limited interest rates on savings accounts. By investing only in short-term debt instruments like Treasury bills and jumbo CDs, such a fund, while not insured by the FDIC, would be almost as safe as a bank savings account and could offer a much higher interest rate. Building upon this inspiration, in early 1970 Brown and Bent submitted for SEC approval the earliest prospectus for a money market fund, or what they then called a "cash management vehicle."

On the West Coast, another innovative fund was being developed around the same time. In January 1970, San Francisco broker James Benham was struck by the long lines of people waiting to buy Treasury bills at the Federal Reserve Bank of San Francisco. One attraction of T-bills was that they were available for a minimum $1,000 purchase, a manageable amount for many smaller investors seeking a safe investment alternative to a bank savings account. But in February 1970, the Treasury Department abruptly raised the minimum purchase amount for T-bills to the lofty sum of $10,000, which instantly excluded many small investors. Sensing both a great business opportunity and an altruistic way to help the small investor, Benham formed Capital Preservation Fund that would invest only in short-term Treasuries and would require a minimum investment of only $1,000. In 1971 he submitted the prospectus for his fund to the SEC for approval.

The SEC took a long time to decide what to do with these curious, newfangled funds, but in September 1972 it finally approved both. Neither fund caught on until a flamboyant salesman/money manager from Pittsburgh, Pennsylvania, named Glen Johnson (no relation to Charlie) popularized the term "money market fund." Glen Johnson was interviewed by scores of newspapers and magazines and appeared on a number of popular network television programs to extol the advantages of money market funds. These marketing efforts quickly expanded the awareness of money market funds from corporate accounting offices (which used them to manage short-term funds) to a growing number of enthusiastic individual investors.

Check-writing privileges, introduced by Fidelity in 1974, increased the popularity of money market funds even more. This innovation shocked many fund managers who were already concerned by the low profit margins possible on money market funds. The check-writing money market fund also angered bankers who feared the loss of their unique and privileged position in the market.

Franklin did not join the money market bandwagon right away. When Lou Woodworth, later a member of Franklin Resources' Board of Directors, initially suggested the idea, Charlie resisted it. Money market funds had no upfront sales charge. "How can we sell a no-load fund?" he asked, expressing concern that this would endanger the company's relationship with brokers. Furthermore, Franklin already offered a safe yet relatively high-interest bond fund that focused on government securities. As the check-writing option grew more popular, however, Franklin realized the importance of money market funds for attracting investors during down markets. These investors could then be directed to other investments as markets recovered.

⮑A month after interest rates had reached historic highs in January 1976, Franklin opened its Liquid Assets Fund. The fund incorporated some of the best ideas from the existing products on the market, but Franklin also added other incentives for investors. For example, most funds had a two-day waiting period on deposits before they started earning interest. Franklin's fund offered interest starting from the day of deposit. To distinguish its fund in an increasingly crowded field, and its own reputation as a company that was friendly to small investors, Franklin established a $500 minimum initial investment for the fund, one of the lowest minimums in the industry. Franklin also took the unusual step of advertising the new fund directly to investors.

⮑"It seems funny today," Charlie says, "but nobody really could figure out where this business was going." Many brokers weren't interested in the fund. At the E. F. Hutton office a block away from Franklin, brokers with customers who wanted to buy money fund shares simply directed them to Franklin's office. To encourage this practice, Franklin began paying brokers $10 per account for referrals. Many brokers soon realized that if they helped investors get started with money market funds, they could build a relationship that would eventually lead to other business as well.

⮑Andy Johnson often appeared on a local Saturday morning radio show, where he talked about money funds and became known as "the Money Doctor." Franklin added staff to open accounts on Saturday mornings and to take the checks that people brought to the door. "It got crazy," remembers Ken Koskella. "Sometimes we would get the mail and open an envelope and there would be a check, just a check." To handle the growing volume of business, Franklin took additional space in the building at Bovet Road and established a retail operation for walk-in customers.

⮑After the 1975 peaks, interest rates fell steadily during the following year. Yet to the surprise of market observers, assets held in money market funds did not fall by the end of 1976. Instead, they continued to rise. Investors increasingly saw money market funds as not just a temporary alternative to banks, but as both a savings vehicle and a tool that enabled them to easily shift money between other types of mutual funds based on the economic environment.

Money funds forced Franklin to think differently about customer service. For the first time the company had a much more direct relationship with customers. "You didn't have a broker/dealer to take their phone calls," Harmon Burns recalls. "So we had to have an ever-growing group of people to handle the calls."

"A lot of people thought we were a bank," says Rupert, Jr. "They would bring a check, and they would ask for change back." Some customers would arrive with cash and had to be told that Franklin couldn't take cash. According to Charlie, "We would make them go down to a bank and get a bank check." No one was complaining, though. At Franklin and other mutual fund firms, money funds played a crucial part in the reinvigoration of an industry that had been in a tailspin.

For the Franklin team, the end of the miserable 1970s couldn't come soon enough. Hard times had taught important lessons. The company had learned to innovate and to follow investors as they followed the markets. It had taken risks on new businesses, not all of which had paid off. But there was no finger-pointing; the company cut its losses and moved on. Tight budgets and cost-cutting had given the Franklin team confidence that they could adjust and reconfigure to survive. As the decade came to a close, Charlie was already beginning to sense the next challenge that would face the company: how to ride the bull as it came out of the chute and not get thrown to the ground or trampled.

CHAPTER III

The Bull Starts Running

Happier days ahead: In March 1982, Franklin board members and friends gather after a meeting at the Peninsula Golf Club in San Mateo. (L-R): Lou Gerald, Murray Simpson, Charlie Johnson, Vince Rigoni, Lou Woodworth, Bob McCullough, Sam Morse, Andy Johnson and Rupert Johnson, Jr.

Opposite: In April 1978, a record trading day on the New York Stock Exchange marked the beginning of the end of the long bear market.

The
Bull Starts Running

Lost time is never found again.

- BENJAMIN FRANKLIN

U.S. President
Ronald Reagan

The inflation-driven 1970s, which fueled investor demand for fixed income securities that would pay high interest rates, helped Franklin find its niche. By 1980 the company had turned a corner. Over the next six years, assets under management and income doubled or nearly doubled every year. Franklin was determined to keep customers happy by meeting their expectations for superior investment performance and service. But keeping pace with rising demand posed serious operational challenges that had the potential to derail the company's success.

    A combination of economic factors and policy changes contributed to the growth of Franklin and the mutual fund industry in the 1980s. New rules and regulations stimulated competition between financial institutions, while changes in government programs provided new tax incentives for Americans to save for retirement and college education. After the dismal performance of the 1970s' markets, what investors wanted most of all was safety. Franklin was well positioned to meet this demand.

THE END OF STAGFLATION

At the outset, few investors anticipated that the 1980s would be any better than the difficult 1970s. The early part of the decade was marked by the frightening possibility of continued inflation without any economic growth, or what some called "stagflation." In a desperate attempt to beat back inflation, the new Federal Reserve chairman, Paul Volcker, launched an extremely tight money policy. Initially, the policy failed to lower inflation, but was quite effective at raising interest rates. The numbers from 1980 were shocking: The prime rate rose to 19 percent, the inflation rate neared 17 percent, and unemployment climbed to almost 8 percent. Meanwhile, the stock market remained stagnant, and the GNP dropped 1 percent. With Ronald Reagan repeatedly asking, "Are you better off than you were four years ago?" few people were surprised when President Jimmy Carter lost his bid for reelection.

Yet among experienced stock analysts, there was a good deal of optimism about the equities market. Price-to-earnings ratios were at record lows and had been for some time. Charlie Johnson indicated as far back as 1977 that the time was right to start investing in stocks again. As he put it, "The downside risk is minimal, and the upside potential could be explosive." As stocks remained historically low in 1981, investor John Templeton sent his fund shareholders a phonograph record with a message about how domestic stocks were significantly undervalued. Those who acted on this message finally saw their financial statements come to life the next year. The market started rising; in October 1982, the Dow Jones Industrial Average passed 1,000 and reached its highest point in a decade. By the end of the year, the press began announcing (still with more hope than certainty) the arrival of a new bull market, the first one since the great postwar bull market had ended in 1966.

THE CHANGING COMPETITIVE LANDSCAPE

As the Federal Reserve worked to bring interest rates under control in the early 1980s, the Reagan administration accelerated the move toward deregulation begun by the Ford and Carter administrations. For years, legislation passed during the Great Depression had separated the securities and banking industries. While banks and savings and loans competed with one another for savings accounts, they rarely targeted investors buying stocks and bonds. The rise of money market funds in the late 1970s blurred these lines. Under pressure from the banking and thrift industries, Congress passed new laws that phased in the elimination of restrictions on passbook savings accounts and gave banks and savings and loans a greater ability to compete with money market funds.

     The decontrol of interest rates offered on savings accounts posed a major competitive threat to Franklin and the mutual fund industry. Following the implementation of the new rules in December 1982, assets in money market funds dropped 16 percent in two months. Funds in markets where banks were especially aggressive, including California, were hit the hardest. Under new competitive pressure, Franklin and other mutual funds responded by expanding the range of their product offerings.

     While regulatory changes posed new competitive threats, revisions to the tax laws created new opportunities. The Economic Recovery Tax Act of 1981, which loosened the rules governing IRAs, encouraged a significant expansion in the mutual fund industry in the 1980s. New rules allowed any wage earner, with or without a pension plan, to open an IRA, and raised the maximum allowable yearly contribution to $2,000. Over the next several years, IRA money poured into fixed income investments at six times the rate of stock funds. Between 1982 and 1986, total assets invested industrywide in mutual fund IRAs increased ninefold, rising from $6 billion to $54 billion.

     Growth of the mutual fund industry in the 1980s was also propelled by the increasing tendency of fund companies to sell directly to investors, rather than through brokers. This trend was accelerated in October 1980, when the SEC approved a new rule that allowed funds to charge existing shareholders a fee for marketing and distribution. The direct-marketed (or "no-load") fund companies were especially eager to see Rule 12b-1 adopted because it provided a way to pay for their advertising and distribution costs.

Economic recovery, combined with new policies that promoted savings and investment and increased competition and advertising, fueled the tremendous growth of the mutual fund industry in the 1980s. Innovation also played an important role in the recovery of the mutual fund industry, and here too Franklin positioned itself for success.

⁀While the money market fund that Franklin launched in 1976 helped the company survive the decade on strengthened financial footing, it was another bond fund launched in 1977 that became the basis for Franklin's unprecedented growth in the 1980s. Ironically, this fund was initially a big disappointment. Called Franklin Tax-Free Income Fund, it was designed to take advantage of a provision of the Tax Reform Act of 1976

A due diligence meeting in 1986 for E. F. Hutton at Franklin's headquarters at 777 Mariners Island Blvd. Portfolio managers, executives and sales-people educated brokers and financial planners about Franklin's products and services.

that altered the rules regarding the taxation of tax-free bond dividends. Previously, all interest that mutual funds paid to shareholders was considered by the IRS to be a taxable dividend, whether the source of the income was stocks, corporate bonds or government tax-free bonds. The Tax Reform Act of 1976, however, allowed mutual fund income derived from tax-free securities to be "passed through" to fund shareholders and remain tax free. Quick to take advantage of this new provision, the company launched Franklin Tax-Free Income Fund in 1977. Unfortunately, interest rates rose sharply between 1978 and 1981, causing a significant decline in bond prices. Issued at $10 a share, Franklin's Tax-Free Income Fund declined to less than $6 per share by 1982.

In the face of these disappointing results, however, an innovative idea was born: Why not experiment by turning the federal tax-free fund into a state-specific, tax-free fund for investors in Franklin's own backyard, California? This would give investors a whole new reason to buy into the fund by offering income that was free from both state and federal taxes. The only problem with this idea was that California did not have the same tax-free "pass-through" rules that now existed at the federal level. Andy Johnson worked with the fund's board of directors and the leadership in the California legislature to pass a new law that aligned the state with the federal statute. Their effort was a success, and a new type

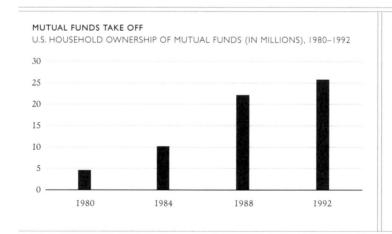

MUTUAL FUNDS TAKE OFF
U.S. HOUSEHOLD OWNERSHIP OF MUTUAL FUNDS (IN MILLIONS), 1980–1992

In the late 1970s, millions of Americans were introduced to mutual funds through money market funds. From 1980 to 1992, the number of households that owned mutual funds increased from 5 million to more than 25 million.

of mutual fund was born. Franklin Tax-Free Income Fund was converted into a fund investing only in California tax-free securities and was renamed Franklin California Tax-Free Income Fund.

As short-term rates significantly declined, money fund shareholders looked for ways to lock in high yields. Franklin California Tax-Free Income Fund and Franklin U.S. Government Securities Fund provided the ideal vehicles, and sales of these two funds exploded. Tom Cotter, Franklin's wholesaler for the western region, was particularly excited by the idea of a California tax-free fund, comparing it to the discovery of the Comstock Lode that launched the California Gold Rush. Cotter and Harry Kline, another Franklin wholesaler, pushed to lower the front-end commission on these funds from 7.25 percent to 4 percent to make them even more attractive to investors. By lowering the upfront cost, brokers significantly increased their sales and ended up making more money.

The timing of Franklin's California tax-free initiative was critical. Facing increased competition from banks, Franklin's promotion of the California tax-free fund helped increase assets in the fund by $784 million between March 1982 and March 1983, to a total of $829 million. Later the same year, the fund reached the $1 billion mark. By September 1987, it had grown to over $6 billion. By early 1993, assets under management in this fund alone reached $13 billion.

Franklin California Tax-Free Income Fund was so successful that some people started calling it "Jaws" because the Franklin muni managers would buy entire issues of tax-free bonds. With that much buying power, Franklin could negotiate much better rates for its fund shareholders. Franklin's team became well known in the industry for being thorough and tough. "The group had a unique personality that reflected Andy's personality and approach," said Harmon Burns.

With success in California, Franklin expanded the tax-free concept to New York and began to look at other states as well. After some debate about what state to enter next, the Franklin team decided to start a fund in every state. At the time, Charlie recalls, "It seemed like a radical

"JAWS" AND THE MUNICIPAL BOND DEPARTMENT

Veteran trader Greg Harrington had retired after a long and successful career in the bond industry, but that didn't stop Andy Johnson from recruiting him to Franklin. Swamped by demand for the newly created Franklin California Tax-Free Income Fund, Andy asked Harrington to help build Franklin's new Municipal Bond Department.

The two industry veterans recruited other veterans and a cadre of young college grads from Franklin's Management Training Program. "We didn't know anything about bonds when we started," says Rafael Costas. The veterans mentored the young recruits. "We learned from the stories they told," says Tom Walsh. "This was the best way to learn," says Sheila Amoroso, "because there was no way to learn about the bond market without being entrenched in it."

The muni team worked hard and played hard. By 1986 the team was so successful that the Franklin California Tax-Free Income Fund was dubbed "Jaws," because it bought such a large percentage of the municipal bonds issued in California.

Franklin California Tax-Free Income Fund was dubbed "Jaws" because it devoured most of the municipal bonds issued in the state. The Municipal Bond Department decorated its offices with this mascot.

idea—let's start one everywhere." But Franklin had come a long way from the hard years of the 1970s. The company now had the resources and record of success to follow through with such an ambitious idea. As the different state funds were developed, a surprising discovery was made: The attraction of these funds was not solely that they provided the unique experience of a monthly tax-free dividend check. People who lived in states like Florida or Texas, which did not have an income tax, also wanted access to a bond fund from their state. As Charlie puts it, "People thought 'I live in Texas. I want Texas bonds.' 'I live in Florida. I want to own Florida bonds.' It had a big market." One by one, Franklin rolled out different state tax-free funds.

Meanwhile, Franklin U.S. Government Securities Fund was another big beneficiary of the rush to lock in high income. In 1983, as money market rates began to decline, Franklin switched the focus of this fund from long-term U.S. government bonds to Government National Mortgage Association mortgage pools. These "Ginnie Maes" offered a higher yield of about 12 percent and the payment of principal and interest was guaranteed by the U.S. government. Franklin was the first to devise a way to offer Ginnie Maes in a mutual fund, and the response was nothing short of astounding. From

N.Y. Tax-Free Income Fund ad January 1986

February 1983, when the fund made the switch, to September 1983, the fund grew from $14 million in assets to over $200 million. By March 1985, when the fund was still offering a 12 percent yield, the fund had total assets under management exceeding $3 billion. In a press release announcing this achievement, Charlie encapsulated the general trend in

Franklin's Municipal Bond Research Team grew from two to 17 people between 1986 and 1992. Under Director Tom Kenny (far left), the group was recognized as one of the top 10 research teams in the U.S. Greg Harrington (far right) and Andy Johnson (second from right) mentored many members of the team, including Tom.

fund investing in the first half of the 1980s by saying, "For most of their history, stock funds have been the dominant force among mutual funds. The record set by Franklin U.S. Government Securities Fund reflects investors' desire for high income with a high degree of safety."

MANAGING THE GROWTH

The success of tax-free, Ginnie Mae and money funds led to exponential growth for Franklin. In September 1981, the company closed its fiscal year with assets under management up 157 percent, from $515 million to $1.3 billion. The following year, and for every year through 1986, assets and net income doubled again.

꒦Franklin faced multiple challenges to keep up with this growth. To gain efficiencies and greater control over customer service, Franklin once again moved to establish its own transfer agency. In 1981 the company created Franklin Administrative Services. As Charlie told shareholders in the fall of 1981, the new organization would allow Franklin

Industry collaboration led to the creation of Fund/SERV, an automated order entry, clearance and settlement system developed in 1986. Franklin's Transfer Agent Manager Frank Isola (second from left) played an important role in the development of this new system.

to directly control the level of service to fund shareholders.

⌐Charlie asked Harmon Burns to develop and supervise the new organization. Burns hired Frank Isola, a longtime employee at Applied Financial Systems, to run the new, wholly owned subsidiary. Internalizing the transfer operation shifted employees from AFS to Franklin. Suddenly, the company's staff jumped from 40 people to more than 100.

⌐Growing demand for Franklin funds required service innovations. When the California fund was first created, trades were taken over the phone, then an agent wrote up the order. The next day, the price and shares information was confirmed back to the broker by telephone, and the broker was sent a paper trade-confirmation invoice. Upon receipt, the broker cut a settlement check and provided Franklin with transfer instructions that enabled Franklin to register shares in the customer's name. According to Isola, "The process resulted in lots of errors." As trading volumes rose from roughly a dozen a day in the late 1970s to hundreds and even thousands of trades a day, Franklin was forced to revamp its back-office operations.

⌐It took AFS more than a year to rewrite its wire order trading system to more efficiently track and record Franklin's

HARMON BURNS

Sue Burns sometimes joked that her husband, Harmon, took the job at Winfield and Co. in California because he wanted to live where baseball star Willie Mays played center field for the San Francisco Giants. An avid sports fan, Harmon Burns was also a savvy businessman who, like Willie Mays, had a solid work ethic and a reputation for good humor.

As Franklin Resources grew beyond anyone's expectations in the 1980s, Burns shouldered enormous responsibilities. After putting himself through law school at night while working for Franklin in the 1970s, he supervised the company's Legal and Compliance Department. He was also the company's chief operating officer and oversaw the rapid expansion of Franklin's customer service and transfer agent operations.

"He always had very good judgment," says Charlie Johnson, "and I very much valued his insights and opinions."

Burns was also a well-respected and well-liked mentor to many of the new college graduates who filled Franklin's middle management ranks in the 1980s.

trades. With some funds paying monthly dividends, the number of accounting entries grew substantially. "We had trade settlement timing delays," Isola recalls. "Dividends had to be adjusted." In addition, many investors wanted a monthly cash dividend check. "To my knowledge, no other financial institution was issuing nearly 100,000 checks a month in a single run, and doing it on a monthly basis," says Isola.

⸞At the forefront of managing this level of daily volume, Franklin had to innovate. In the mid-1980s, the company relied on high-speed IBM laser printers to produce checks and create a highly reliable tape for bank reconciliation purposes. When Xerox came out with a new laser printer that used magnetic ink toner, Franklin was the first to embrace this new technology. Checks were printed in-house under contract with a service management firm. When Franklin converted its government fund to Ginnie Mae securities, orders exploded again. "We were suddenly opening hundreds and sometimes more than a thousand accounts a day," Isola recalls. Finding the people to handle and manage all of this business became critical to Franklin's continued success.

FINDING PEOPLE, MOLDING MANAGERS

As Franklin grew in the 1980s, employees from all walks of life and many different cultural backgrounds joined the company. A core group of employees in the transfer agency had roots in the islands of Tonga and Samoa. Many of them had been recruited to Franklin by Judy Faasisila, who had started with the transfer agency when it was still with AFS. A leader in her community, Faasisila exerted a powerful influence on the job as well. "There was a kinship among the people who worked there," remembers Deborah Gatzek. "People took their jobs very seriously and really felt that service was important."

⸞Increasingly, Franklin needed to build a talent pipeline that the company could draw upon as the business grew. Both Charlie Johnson and Harmon Burns felt a college education set an important foundation for career success, and they also felt strongly about promoting from within whenever possible. Mid-career graduates with experience were expensive, especially during boom times in the Bay Area. Instead, Franklin opted to recruit new college graduates and train them to meet the company's growing need for mid-level managers. The company also established a Tuition Assistance Program to encourage current employees to pursue college degree courses.

⌁Penny Alexander (then Penny Stack) was emblematic of the new, young talent Franklin needed to run its fast-growing business. When she first arrived at Franklin, she wasn't even sure she wanted the job. Newly graduated from the University of Santa Clara in 1982, she had spent the previous several months traveling through Europe wearing jeans and carrying a backpack. After months on the road, she felt out of character sitting in the reception area on the sixth floor at Bovet Road in San Mateo wearing a blue suit with a bow tie.

⌁On that day in November, Alexander was directed into Human Resources where she took a written aptitude test. Then she was interviewed by the department head, Donna Ikeda. To her surprise, Ikeda offered her a job on the spot and asked if she could start right away. Alexander panicked, still unprepared mentally for the idea of a full-time job. "I can't do it now," she told Ikeda. "But I can start on Monday." At home, her mother was delighted with the news, but Alexander wondered what she had gotten herself into.

Employees of the month (EOM Program) assembled for Franklin Resources' *1985 Annual Report.*

In her first year on the job, Alexander came to appreciate how Franklin's leadership shaped the organization's culture. One day, for example, she was on a call. "Someone was at lunch or on break and the phones were ringing. Out of the corner of my eye I saw someone kind of barrel down the hall and grab the phone." Alexander remembers hearing, "'This is Shareholder Services, Charlie speaking, how can I help you?'" Charlie Johnson then spent some time with the customer, hunting and pecking on the keyboard to get the answers to the customer's questions. A new employee, Alexander expected the boss to be angry when he hung up. "When things slowed down, he just returned to his office. No fanfare." Moments like these convinced Alexander that she wanted to stay with Franklin. After a year on the job, she was invited to join the company's newly created Management Training Program.

Basil Fox entered the Management Training Program in its second year. Recruited in 1984 from the University of San Francisco where he was finishing an undergraduate degree in business, Fox met with Ikeda when she visited the campus. Ikeda talked to Fox about Franklin's business, the Johnson family and the strong culture Charlie and Rupert, Jr., had created within the organization. Fox was impressed, applied for a position and was accepted. "We sort of stood out within the organization," he remembers. "We were the college kids, wearing ties." Many of these new

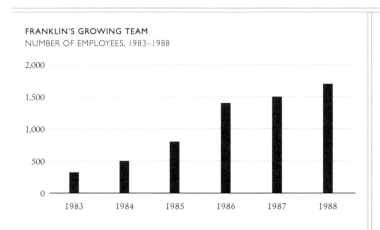

FRANKLIN'S GROWING TEAM
NUMBER OF EMPLOYEES, 1983–1988

As demand for Franklin's funds surged in the 1980s, hundreds of new employees joined the company. The Management Training Program provided many with opportunities to advance their careers.

employees became friends as well as co-workers. They formed sports teams. For those "who wanted to distinguish themselves," Fox says, there were plenty of opportunities. Meanwhile, after work, Franklin employees, including Charlie, Rupert, Jr., and Harmon Burns, would often gather at Chuck's Steakhouse on Bovet Road to unwind and socialize.

The Management Training Program played a critical role in developing the mid-level leadership that would help Franklin grow. His first day on the job, Fox remembers that Charlie, Rupert, Jr., and Harmon Burns took turns speaking to the trainees. Charlie asked the new employees why they had decided to enter the mutual fund industry. "A large majority of the 12 of us wanted to become a portfolio manager," Fox remembers. "And Charlie responded, 'Well that's interesting, but I'd like to point out to you that a minority of the people here are actually involved in money management, and a very important part of what we do is take care of customers.'"

As more managers supervised a growing staff of employees, Charlie also recognized that he had to delegate more. From the time the company had moved to California, he had entrusted Rupert, Jr., with the investment side of the business, and the portfolio managers reported to him. Always even-keeled, "Rupert might be wildly disappointed in somebody," recalls one longtime associate, "but I never saw him lose his temper." Like Charlie, he maintained a high ethical standard.

By the early 1980s, Charlie increasingly relied on Burns to oversee operations. "By that time I had worked with Harmon for seven years," says Charlie, "and I can't remember a time that I didn't agree with his judgment." Increasingly, Burns was the one who was bringing different parts of the organization together, ensuring that there was good communication across the different departments. Employees respected him because he was smart and good-natured. Burns joined Charlie and Rupert for conversations that would shape the future of the business.

Another sign of the changes taking place came in 1983 when Burns went looking for an attorney to help the company with prospectuses for funds, legal review of advertising, human resource and other general business issues. A mutual friend put him in touch with Deborah Gatzek. Bright and energetic, Gatzek had worked for the SEC in the mid-1970s before she and her husband, Les Kratter, moved to the Bay Area. She then served with the National Association of Securities Dealers (NASD) and "was their only attorney west of the Mississippi" for a long time. After she had her first child in 1980, the travel for this job became a burden. When Burns contacted her, she welcomed the opportunity to take what she thought was going to be a "part-time" position as in-house counsel. For Franklin, the opportunity to hire an attorney with such an extraordinary regulatory background was a major accomplishment.

⏪Personally, Charlie began to shift gears. When the company was small, everyone felt comfortable coming to him directly with a concern. He didn't want to lose that culture. The demands on his time were increasing exponentially, but he made sure to get out into the offices, to

Harmon Burns oversaw operations through the 1980s as senior vice president. He exemplified the culture of thriftiness and service, which he saw as cornerstones of Franklin's success.

listen to people taking the phone calls from customers. He continued to be a very approachable senior executive.

⁀During these years, as Ann remembers, "He would come home from work late, and then run." On weekends, he would leave the house and run 20 miles on the roads and trails of the Peninsula. In 1982 and 1983, he and his son Chuck completed several marathons. Charlie found the workouts "invigorating." They also gave him perspective on the business. As his children were growing up, Charlie also began to think of the role they might play in the business.

A NEW GENERATION COMES OF AGE

For the seven children of Ann and Charlie Johnson, Franklin was where their father worked, but it did not dominate their childhoods. Their primary connection with their father was through sports and chores. Saturdays in New Jersey, Charlie took his sons to hockey practice early. After the family moved to California, Charlie coached his youngest daughter's soccer team because "they didn't have enough coaches, and somebody had to do it. And the team won," Ann remembers. As a coach, "He was very strict, but he was good." Charlie himself played tennis,

DEBORAH GATZEK

As an NASD attorney with a young family, Deborah Gatzek decided to take a job with Franklin Resources because she wanted a saner schedule with less business travel.

The job turned out to be anything but slow-paced. Working for Harmon Burns, Gatzek handled prospectuses, advertising and blue-sky issues. Eventually, she became the highest-ranking woman in the company.

Gatzek came to appreciate the integrity of Franklin's leadership. On one occasion, the company discovered that one of its funds had a significant position that had been mispriced by a third party for some time. Gatzek determined that Franklin was not legally liable. When she talked to Charlie Johnson, she says, "He didn't spend more than two or three minutes looking at the numbers, and immediately perceived a pattern in the pricing relationships that we should have noticed on our own." Gatzek recalls that Charlie didn't hesitate. "We're going to pay this," he said. "Our people should have picked this up."

frequently with the boys, and also played handball. On the court he often quietly imparted the values he believed would strengthen his children in business. "I remember playing with him in a doubles tournament," says Charlie's son Greg, "and I was probably getting a little too animated or angry when I missed a shot. He stopped and said, 'One more outburst and we're walking off the court, and I'm not playing with you anymore.' That was it. That was all he had to say."

One business lesson Charlie did bring home was financial prudence, which he often stressed with his children. "You were always going to know the value of a dollar," Greg remembers. For extra spending money, there was always extra work in the garden. "He made it clear that there was a direct connection between work and reward." As they reached their teenage years, if the Johnson children wanted a car to drive, they had to buy it on their own. Neither Charlie nor Ann pressured the children to work for Franklin. "I assume people are going to decide what they want to do," Ann says, "so we never really pushed them to do anything." Charlie and Ann preferred to be an example to their children. As they reached their teenage years, Charlie's children understood that they were welcome to come into the business. "I told them there was no favoritism. They would have to prove themselves and work hard." Or, as Charlie's daughter Jenny put it, he said, "Look, you come work for the company, you work harder than everybody else because the expectations on you are much greater. You're going to be under a magnifying glass, and you're also setting an example. People will look to you, and if you're not working harder than everybody else, they think they don't have to work quite as hard."

At one time or another, all of Charlie and Ann's children worked at least for a summer in the business. Sarah, Holly and Bill ultimately chose other pursuits. Sadly, their youngest daughter, Mary, passed away from a pulmonary embolism in 1990. Chuck, Greg and Jenny, however, came back to make their careers with Franklin after tasting life in other corporate environments. All three say they never felt pressured by their father to work for the company, but life at home created what Jenny described as "a tremendous desire to work in the business." If they joined the business, Charlie insisted that his children "show him and everyone else what they could do before they moved up," as Franklin's longtime legal advisor Murray Simpson put it. Nevertheless, they also enjoyed Charlie's quiet confidence that, if given the opportunity, they would indeed demonstrate their value.

꜀As the oldest, Chuck was the first to start full-time with Franklin. After high school, he had enrolled at UCLA to study economics. Through college he worked at McDonald's and then as a short-order cook in a restaurant to pay for his own expenses. When he graduated, he took a job with the accounting firm of Coopers & Lybrand. Two years later, after working on numerous audits, he passed the CPA exam in 1981. At that point, he decided he was ready to come to work for Franklin.

꜀Chuck started in the trading room, but soon moved to the order room where he contributed to Franklin's phenomenal growth boom. When the bond funds hit, Chuck remembers, "We were doing 50 trades a day, and then all of a sudden that escalated to 500 a day over about a two-month period." Early in his career, Chuck played the key role in bringing Franklin into the age of the personal computer. Driving to work one day, he

The Johnson family, 1977. Standing (L-R): Bill, Mary, Chuck, Charlie, Jenny and Greg. Seated (L-R): Holly, Ann and Sarah.

stopped at an IBM store and "walked in and bought an IBM portable computer." Carrying the machine into his office, Chuck began reading the DOS manual. Soon, the order room was using the machine to log trades in an early and popular program called dBASE. "It was unbelievable. For the first time we could sort our trades by broker, by quantity or by date." When the old guard first spotted the arrival of computers in Franklin's offices, some were wary of what it might mean for the company. Martin Wiskemann was heard to say, "There goes my retirement down the drain." According to Ed Jamieson, Wiskemann thought computers would mean "the end of Franklin" because the company would just end up spending all its resources on technology. After two years with Franklin, Chuck moved east to Massachusetts to complete an M.B.A. at Harvard.

Greg initially planned to attend UCLA like his brother, but Chuck encouraged him to try a smaller school. He chose Washington and Lee University in Virginia, where Rupert, Jr., had gone. Greg followed in his brother's footsteps after college, when he too went to work for Coopers & Lybrand. This decision was partly a result of Charlie's influence. He advised his children with an interest in the financial business to first learn

Chuck Johnson joined Franklin in 1981 after completing a degree in economics at UCLA and spending two years in public accounting. While working in the order room, he bought Franklin's first personal computer, signaling a new era.

accounting by working for an accounting firm. After two and a half years at Coopers & Lybrand, Greg decided he was ready to join Franklin.

⌒Greg started working on Ginnie Mae reconciliations in 1985, but soon moved to the trading desk. Rising every morning just after 4:00 a.m. to be at work when the markets opened in New York "... was a challenge to your social life," he remembers, "but it really gave you a good sense of how the overall capital markets worked." From time to time while Greg was working this job, Charlie would ask him to look at various corporate bonds he was considering for Franklin Income Fund. Soon he was named the co-manager with his father of Franklin Utilities Fund and Franklin Income Fund. These were, in many ways, the flagship funds of the company started by his grandfather, Rupert, Sr. For Greg it was a rite of passage. As a portfolio manager, he enjoyed the implicit competition and also experienced the pressure. "Your performance is measured every day," he says.

⌒After Chuck graduated from Harvard and returned to Franklin, he took over marketing and worked to draw Greg into that side of the business. "I remember a meeting with Ed McVey, our sales manager at the time, and Chuck," Greg recalls. "They wanted me to join their team. I said, 'Why would I want to go into sales?' They both said, 'That's where the rubber hits the road.'" Greg soon discovered the truth of this logic. In sales and marketing he came to appreciate that the success of any mutual fund company depends on three basic ingredients: investment performance, service and sales. "Performance is one thing," he says, "but if you don't have the relationships and can't get the message out to the key people, it's like a tree falling in the forest. It's not going to be heard."

⌒Like her brothers, Jenny was also competitive. She was recruited to play basketball for the University of California at Davis. After graduating, she entered Drexel Burnham's management training program in New York, where she rotated through various parts of the operation, including the trading and options floors. After a year in New York, she came back to California and began working for Franklin in July 1988, apprenticing under Burns. Thus by the late 1980s, a younger generation of Johnsons had begun their on-the-job training at Franklin, becoming part of a larger team focused on the company's continued growth and expansion.

A NEW BUILDING AND BEN

By the mid-1980s Franklin's coming of age was evident in many ways. In 1985 *Forbes* recognized Franklin Resources as the best-performing small company in the United States. Total assets under management crossed the $10 billion mark on June 21, 1985. Franklin's market share in the mutual fund industry rose from 0.6 percent in 1981 to 4.5 percent in 1986. Phenomenal business growth had increased the number of employees to over 1,000. The company moved from its longtime headquarters on Bovet Road to a brand-new building at 777 Mariners Island Boulevard in 1986. The move brought a deep change in the culture. The offices on Bovet Road were spartan and contributed to a feeling that the business was always on the edge financially. At Mariners Island, people had the sense "that the company wasn't going to go away," says Deborah Gatzek. "It could pay its bills. It was a good place to work."

When Franklin Resources began trading on the New York Stock Exchange in 1986, people in the industry also realized that Franklin was a force to be reckoned with. As the company prepared for its entry onto the big board, management discussed what symbol to use. Jerry Palmieri

In 1986, with a growing staff and business, Franklin moved its headquarters to 777 Mariners Island Blvd. in San Mateo.

suggested the symbol BEN to Rupert, Jr. Another company had been using the BEN symbol, but it went bankrupt. "It scares me," Rupert told Palmieri, thinking it might be bad luck. On the other hand, BEN's availability at just the right time could also be read as a good omen.

Greater visibility in the industry brought its own challenges. It was one thing to swim beneath the surface, out of the view of the harpoonists. As Franklin came to the surface with recognition in the national press, it risked becoming the spouting whale. "All of a sudden people became aware of the tremendous growth that we were having," recalls Charlie, "and they started copying us." Charlie, however, didn't see this as the biggest competitive threat in the mid-1980s. He was more worried about Franklin's heavy emphasis on fixed income investments, which had become the company's "bread and butter." As Charlie said, "The biggest risk we faced was from a bull market in common stocks." Just as the equities market was starting to take off, however, a sudden stumble sent many investors running for shelter.

THE CRASH OF 1987

The bull market of the 1980s began to show signs of weakness as early as the spring of 1987. Warren Buffett, for example, announced that the stock market was overpriced and decided to put $700 million in medium-term, tax-exempt bonds rather than buy equities. Meanwhile, the Dow continued

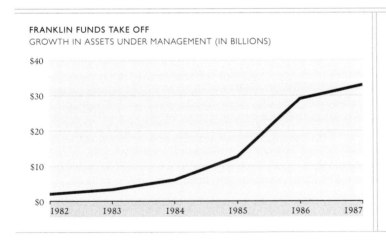

FRANKLIN FUNDS TAKE OFF
GROWTH IN ASSETS UNDER MANAGEMENT (IN BILLIONS)

The popularity of money funds, coupled with the success of Franklin's series of tax-free income funds, led to spectacular growth. Assets under management grew from $2 billion to more than $33 billion between 1982 and 1987.

Franklin's corporate shares began trading as "BEN" on the New York Stock Exchange on December 5, 1986. Gathered on the floor of the exchange to mark the opening day of trading (L-R): Jerry Palmieri, Lou Gerald, Rupert H. Johnson, Jr., Charlie Johnson and John R. Wierdama, the specialist in Franklin stock.

to rise. By August, with shares trading at nearly 20 times earnings, the Dow hit an all-time high of 2,722, but as summer turned to fall, investors grew uneasy. When Congress opened hearings on corporate securities in October, financial news headlines focused on the forays of corporate raiders like Ivan Boesky, Carl Icahn and James Goldsmith. In the Democrat-controlled Congress, the Democratic caucus of the House Ways and Means Committee agreed to add new anti-takeover provisions to the tax laws. Some market analysts have suggested that this move triggered a 10 percent decline in stock prices over the next three days.

⌁ On Monday, October 19, the pace of business on the phones picked up. "You could feel this thing coming," remembers Penny Alexander. "And you couldn't stay on top of the phones." As the panic built, management encouraged customer service agents to have customers call their financial advisors to help calm their fears. As the situation became clear, the company's top managers came together. "You never saw Charlie or Rupert or Harmon flip out," Alexander remembers. "They were very calm. They were focused.... The most important thing was for people to pick up the phone and get us at the other end of the line. We needed to reassure people. 'Yes, this certainly is market fluctuation, but let's keep the long term in mind.'"

⌁ That day the market plunged, falling 508 points, a 22.6 percent drop. From its peak in August, the Dow had lost nearly 1,000 points. In an interview with *Barron's* the next month, Charlie remarked that while watching on his office computer as Franklin's stock declined from $22 a

Gathered for the Franklin "Cruise on the Bay" in May 1988 (L-R): R. Neva Cotter, Charlie Johnson, Dick Stoker, Linda Sender, John Sender, Ann (Mrs. Earl) Johnson, Tom Cotter and Earl Johnson.

WILLIAM LIPPMAN

In 1960 when Bill Lippman announced that he was going to start his own brokerage firm, his boss commented, "That's the most ridiculous thing I've ever heard, but you will be good at it."

Lippman had entered the brokerage business in 1955 as a sales manager for King Merritt & Co., where he reported to Henry Lou Jamieson. When he launched his own company, he named it William Jennings & Co. In 1964 he started Pilgrim Fund, which invested in financial services corporations. Five years later, Lippman took his company public, then oversaw its growth until he sold it in 1984.

Two years later, Lippman agreed to join L. F. Rothschild, Unterberg, Towbin, a venerable bond company in New York, to help launch a series of mutual funds. Lippman and his team created four funds and had $100 million in assets a year later. The market crash of 1987, however, made the parent company decide to sell its mutual fund business. Franklin acquired the company because Charlie had faith in Lippman.

share to around $12, "I began to chuckle. I thought it had almost gotten to the point of being silly." Charlie was confident that Franklin's stock would hold up in the long run. It would take over a year for the stock to return to its pre-crash price, but in a larger way Franklin had dodged a bullet. Because most of the company's investments were income or bond funds, the market crash had little effect on Franklin's products, and indirectly it led to a new opportunity for the company to get some balance on the equities side of the business.

In 1988 Charlie seized an opportunity to forge a tighter working relationship with an associate and friend from his early days in the mutual fund industry. L. F. Rothschild, Unterberg, Towbin, an investment firm with roots stretching back to 1895, had run into financial problems in the year following the plunge in the stock market. To generate cash, they were looking to divest their relatively small mutual fund business, including the four funds then managed by Charlie's longtime friend Bill Lippman. Franklin agreed to acquire the business. Three of the company's funds were merged with other Franklin funds; the fourth, Rising Dividends, continued under Lippman's management.

The market crash thus shaped the economic environment in which Franklin operated and created new opportunities, but two years later the company discovered that Mother Nature had a role to play as well.

THE LESSON OF THE QUAKE

Market quakes were followed by the real thing when the Loma Prieta earthquake rocked the San Francisco Bay Area in October 1989. On that day, a number of Franklin's employees left work in mid-afternoon to watch the third baseball game of the World Series between the Oakland A's and the San Francisco Giants. Harmon Burns was already in the company's box at Candlestick Park, and Greg was on the escalator when the earthquake struck. "People clapped," Greg remembered, "and we just continued on in to watch the game." Then a fan with a portable television showed him news coverage of the collapsed section of the Bay Bridge. Suddenly, Greg realized the gravity of the situation. Around the Bay Area, dozens of people were killed by the damage caused by the quake. Thousands were stranded by the rupture of the lower deck of the Bay Bridge and the collapse of the Cypress Freeway in the East Bay.

At Mariners Island, the few remaining Franklin employees could see smoke rising in the distance. Charlie, who had just had knee

Following the Loma Prieta earthquake in 1989, President George Bush and Congressman George Miller toured the site of the collapsed I-880 Cypress Freeway in Oakland, California. Across the bay, the earthquake caused considerable damage to Franklin's offices at 777 Mariners Island Blvd.

surgery, was still at his desk when the quake struck. With help from his secretary, Marion Eichar, he hobbled down seven flights of stairs to the ground level.

⮌ The next day, employees arrived and began to clean up, but the building manager smelled gas and told everyone to leave. The situation became critical after Franklin's management realized how difficult it would be for the company to complete its daily pricing of the company's funds. Someone called the SEC and explained the situation, but the regulators were not going to budge. They told us, "You're on the phone, therefore you're there, and therefore you've got to price your funds," remembers Basil Fox. Somehow the job got done.

OPENING RANCHO CORDOVA

The quake revealed how vulnerable Franklin was to a disaster. With all of its operations concentrated in a single site in the quake-prone Bay Area, a stronger earthquake could put the company out of business. This sobering realization led to a management team decision to identify a new site for operations. Chuck Johnson asked Fox, who was now a senior manager in the transfer agency, to oversee site selection, construction and development. It was an intimidating assignment. Handed the baton, Basil discovered, "Once people here decide to do something and commit to it, and they entrust you to do it, they are going to give you a lot of latitude to execute it."

⮌ Fox looked at sites in or near Fort Lee, New Jersey; Reno, Nevada; and Sacramento, California. New Jersey was attractive because Bill Lippman was headquartered in Fort Lee, and it made sense to have operations centers located on both coasts. Reno was another option because it was not far from the Bay Area, offered some tax advantages and was seismically stable. In the end, however, Fox recommended Sacramento. "The entire population from Reno through the valley to Carson City was a quarter million," he says, noting that this low labor supply simply would not be sufficient for the pace of hiring that Franklin anticipated. "If we want to do it fast," he told Charlie and Burns, "we have to do it in

Sacramento" with its substantially larger metropolitan population. Fox also recommended Sacramento because it was relatively close to San Mateo. "I felt I could leverage some management people. If I was four hours away from headquarters, it was going to be harder to get them to visit, to do training and things like that." After listening to Fox's report, the executive team accepted his recommendation. For Franklin, this move represented the first step away from the company's home base in San Mateo.

It took nearly three years to complete the building of the new operations center in Rancho Cordova, just outside of Sacramento, but the facility quickly became critical to Franklin's continued growth. Mather Air Force Base had closed at almost the same time the new facility opened, providing a new pool of roughly 1,200 potential employees in the region. Franklin's recruiting process accelerated. By the end of 1993, the staff at Rancho was handling half of all incoming calls from shareholders, investment advisors and the investing public. A third of all work done by Franklin's operations departments flowed out of Rancho Cordova. On the first of December, staff began moving into the second building in the complex, bringing the total number of employees on site up to 350. Basil Fox, however, could hardly take time to savor the moment. Even before the doors had opened, Chuck Johnson had pulled him into a new project that would transform the company.

TEMPLETON

Chapter IV

Becoming
Franklin Templeton

Sir John Templeton addresses a group of fund shareholders in 1985. Templeton was renowned for his trailblazing success in global investing.

Opposite: Templeton headquarters in Nassau, Bahamas.

Becoming
Franklin Templeton

*To succeed, jump as quickly at opportunities
as you do at conclusions.*

~ BENJAMIN FRANKLIN

Despite Franklin's success in the early and mid-1980s, some analysts questioned whether its predominant focus on fixed income investments and relatively few equity fund offerings would start to crimp the company's remarkable growth. In 1986 Rupert Johnson, Jr., told the *San Francisco Chronicle* that he was not overly concerned that Franklin's emphasis on fixed income securities was a problem. Although he admitted, "We're always looking," he suggested that Franklin's collection of seven equity funds was sufficient, and fixed income would remain the company's main focus. "As long as you can offer a rate of return higher than inflation," he said, "you are performing an investment service."

But stock funds were not going to lag behind forever. Starting in the mid-1980s, as the price of shares began to rise and inflation declined, investors once again turned their attention to equity investing. Two trends fueled their interest: the rise of professional fund managers who could help direct investment decisions, and the growing popularity of "diversification" as an investment strategy that promised to reduce the risks of equity investing. The industry itself was also continuing to innovate, offering investors a variety of new funds.

Another trend emerged in the mid-1980s that would affect Franklin and the entire mutual fund world. This was the rise of globalization. In Europe, Asia and Latin America, state-controlled economies began to be transformed in the late 1980s by free-market reforms and the opening of investment opportunities to foreign companies. In addition, the establishment of private pension systems in many countries created a need among ordinary investors for more diverse financial services and products.

Franklin's first steps into the world of global funds can be traced to a chance conversation in 1985, when Chuck Johnson was on vacation in Taiwan after graduating from business school. There he met an employee of another large, American mutual fund company who was visiting the island on business. In the hotel fitness room, the two men struck up a conversation. Chuck took note of the man's answer to his question of how much interest banks paid on savings accounts in Taiwan: "The banks don't pay. They charge."

Puzzled and amazed by this response, Chuck embarked on a quest to understand why banks might actually charge their customers to deposit money. What he learned convinced him that Taiwan, despite its daunting economic and regulatory environment, represented a huge potential opportunity that Franklin could not ignore.

While the man Chuck met at the hotel was exaggerating (people did not commonly pay banks to hold their money), his answer highlighted the nature of Taiwan's financial system up through the late 1980s. On the one hand, Taiwan's economy was booming. Decades of successful government-led economic development had transformed Taiwan into one of the "four tigers" (along with Hong Kong, Singapore and Korea), and the country enjoyed a growing trade surplus with its principal trading partner, the United States. On the other hand, Taiwan was trapped in what has been called a state of "financial repression." The government tightly regulated the financial system as part of its efforts to rapidly develop the country from an agrarian-based society to an industrial powerhouse.

Government restrictions on the financial system left Taiwan's growing middle- and upper-income population with few places to invest. Banks were all state-owned and mainly served the needs of large, often state-owned, industrial enterprises. Interest paid on savings accounts was controlled by the central bank and was usually quite low. Taiwan's stock market was heavily regulated, and few companies were listed. There was a very limited money market, and there were no private brokerages or investment companies. Private foreign investment was also forbidden as the government sought to build up Taiwan's foreign exchange reserves. While the wealthy and well-connected were able to skirt regulations and invest abroad, this too was an increasingly unattractive option. With Taiwan's export-driven growth (the Taiwanese currency appreciated quickly despite the government's best efforts to keep it down), earnings from dollar-denominated investments couldn't keep pace. The Taiwanese government began permitting the establishment of mutual funds in 1985, but at first only three were authorized, and they did little to expand the range of investment options available to Taiwan's citizens.

By the time of Chuck's first visit to Taiwan in 1985, the problem of too much money with too few places to invest was having a significant impact on the island's economy. After returning home to San Mateo, Chuck convinced his father and uncle to expand into Taiwan. Then he persuaded a Taiwanese banker named Frank Liu to leave his secure position in San Francisco to undertake the difficult job of helping Franklin Resources establish an office in Taiwan. Chuck consciously adopted a very low-key strategy. Rather than hire a well-known local figure to open the office, he found in Liu someone who had not yet made his mark but was young, talented and committed to building the business. They kept overhead as low as possible, which gave them the time they needed to become successful.

The office opened in 1986, and in certain respects the timing was perfect. The government was undergoing a rapid period of liberalization and democratization on all fronts. Martial law was lifted in 1987, and free elections were allowed. The government also lifted restrictions on foreign investment, allowing Taiwan's citizens to invest up to $5 million abroad each year. This regulatory shift enabled foreign financial firms like Franklin Resources to register with Taiwan's Securities and Exchange Commission as "licensed securities investment consultants." With this license, they could market mutual funds and other investment products on the island.

Despite these developments, Frank Liu's Franklin office struggled during its first five years in Taiwan. The process of navigating all the regulatory changes the government was instituting was "painful," says Chuck. "There were no rules, there were no laws. You couldn't hire a law firm and say, 'Can I do this?' or 'Should I not do this?' No one would say because the laws were all kind of gray," he recalls. "And the regulators wouldn't say, either." As one example, in 1991 authorities suddenly banned all commercial banks from promoting foreign mutual funds out of an avowed concern over false advertising practices.

Regulatory issues aside, Taiwan's investors were initially not very interested in Franklin's investment options. People were either conservative and hesitant about giving their money to a foreign company they had never heard of, or they were fixated on Taiwan's own domestic real estate and stock market boom. Chuck remembers being turned away by banks unimpressed with the 9 percent yearly return offered by Franklin U.S. Government Securities Fund, because people were earning 4 percent a month from underground investment "companies." By the late 1980s, newspapers reported that people were quitting their day jobs, certain that their money would just keep doubling in the market. Between 1987 and 1988, the Taiwan market rose over 700 percent. Eventually, and inevitably, it all came crashing down. From February to October 1990, the Taiwanese stock market dropped from 12,682 points to 2,485. Just as in other times in Franklin's history, after the bubble burst, people who soberly sought more secure investment options became increasingly interested in what Franklin had to offer.

⁀Starting in the early 1990s, Franklin saw its business begin to grow in Taiwan. Funds from investors began to flow in. By 1992 an analyst report was calling Taiwan "one of the most exciting retail asset management marketplaces in Asia, and one that... holds much promise for the future." At the same time, the analyst warned that time was running out to establish a presence on the island. Fortunately, Franklin was in early, and the company's eventual success in Taiwan suggested possibilities for expanding in Asia and other parts of the world.

THE FIRST MOVE TOWARD INDUSTRY CONSOLIDATION

By the late 1980s, many industry watchers, including Goldman Sachs in New York, began suggesting that a wave of consolidation would soon sweep the mutual fund industry. Improvements in data communications and operations had made it possible to manage both large organizations and large volumes of customer accounts efficiently. As baby boomers began to think seriously about their retirement, significant growth in the industry could occur, and when it did, larger firms would likely benefit. This type of speculation about mergers and consolidation often led to John Templeton's name.

⁀Templeton, Galbraith and Hansberger (TGH) had grown into a mutual fund powerhouse by the early 1990s, but Templeton was increasingly feeling his age and wanted to put more energy into his various charitable works. A deeply religious man (accounts of the annual meetings of Templeton Growth Fund often note their spiritual atmosphere), Templeton's major interest was facilitating research into connections between religion and science. With TGH and its funds so closely identified with one famous man, some expressed concern over the fate of the company once Templeton finally left. Templeton himself had little patience with any negative speculation over the implications of his stepping down. He remarked, "When you go into the Morgan Guaranty Trust Company, you never ask, 'Where's J. P. Morgan?' ... When you come to Templeton International, it's a little out of date to say, 'Where's Templeton?' Ninety-five percent of the work is done by the 500 other people."

By the time Templeton was approaching his 80th birthday in 1991 and his longtime partner John Galbraith was 70, they were increasingly courted by would-be acquirers. "The minute you even smiled," Galbraith says, "all of a sudden you had people chasing you." The interest was hardly surprising. TGH was then the United States' 26th largest mutual fund management company, with around $19 billion in assets in 78 funds and 13 research offices in 10 countries around the world. Templeton had entertained various merger offers since the mid-1980s. But all offers had been rejected, and Templeton's reputation as a notoriously demanding negotiator led many to suspect that TGH would never actually be sold.

Thus when Charlie received a phone call from New York late in 1991, he was skeptical at first. On the line was a former investment banker, who told Charlie that Sir John Templeton was seeking a buyer for his company and was curious to know if Franklin Resources was interested

SIR JOHN TEMPLETON

John Templeton was working for a seismic exploration company when World War II began in Europe. Believing that the war would end the Great Depression at last, he called his broker and told him to buy $100 worth of every stock on the major exchanges that was selling for $1 or less. To make this $10,000 purchase, Templeton had to borrow the money. Four years later, his investment had quadrupled in value, and Templeton used some of the proceeds to go into business as an investment advisor.

Over the next several decades, John Templeton earned a reputation as one of the smartest investors of the 20th century. The farm boy from Tennessee, who was educated at Yale and became a Rhodes scholar, launched Templeton Growth Fund in 1954. Over the next 38 years, the fund averaged a 15 percent annual return.

Noted for his philanthropy and interest in religion, Templeton endowed the Templeton Foundation Prize for Progress in Religion, an award that some soon compared to the Nobel Prize. In 1973 Mother Teresa won the first award.

JOHN GALBRAITH

A pilot in World War II, Galbraith flew commercial planes for six years after the war. He met his wife, Rosemary, a flight attendant, on a blind date. Eventually, they both left aviation to focus on the world of investing. In 1974 Galbraith went to see John Templeton. He told him that Templeton had a great product that needed marketing and sales support. They reached an agreement that led to the creation of Securities Fund Investors, Inc., in 1974.

For four years the company operated out of Saddle River, New Jersey. In 1978 John and Rosemary decided to move the business to St. Petersburg, Florida, to take advantage of good weather, an available workforce and a nearby airport. The Galbraiths bought and restored a historic art deco building to house the company and made it a landmark in St. Petersburg.

in a meeting. After hanging up, Charlie walked over to Chuck's office and asked what he thought. Despite some initial doubts that Templeton was really ready to sell, Charlie knew the possibility had to be pursued. As Charlie said, "We had wanted to diversify for some time." Chuck also pointed out that "firms like Templeton's don't come on the market very often. He's got what we don't: a broad line of equity products, a fantastic track record and an international infrastructure. To survive in the next 10 years, we'll have to be global."

Soon after their conversation, Charlie traveled to meet Templeton. Despite the years that each had spent in the industry, they had never sat down to talk before. "Templeton got right to the point," Charlie recalls. He said he and his partners were thinking of selling. He laid out his terms and named his price. "He was very direct about the whole thing," says Charlie. "There was no kind of sparring." When Charlie returned to San Mateo, he told Chuck, "Why don't you pull together a team and take a look."

Chuck was soon on his way to New York, where he hired the team from Goldman Sachs led by Milton Berlinski. Franklin also needed legal support. When Les Kratter, Deborah Gatzek's husband, volunteered to help Charlie and Chuck pick an appropriate Wall Street law firm, it was the beginning of a long and productive career with the company. Together, Kratter and Chuck flew to Florida where they met Templeton at a hotel near the Miami airport. It was an unforgettable highlight of Chuck's young career. "Here I was, this punk kid, meeting this venerated old Wall Street hand."

An early sign that the prize of TGH would not be easily won came during the first Miami meeting when, as Chuck remembers it, Sir John insisted, "You can only talk to me. I don't want you calling anyone else in my firm." Not only did this make the practical task of completing due diligence difficult, it created a strange atmosphere in which to negotiate. Chuck quickly recognized there were other forces or currents going on in connection with TGH, but could not quite determine what they were. "It was like trying to figure out, in astronomy, that there must be a black hole because of this weird rotation of this planet or something. . . . Things weren't moving the way they normally should in a normal equilibrium." The secrecy surrounding the whole process was unusually intense.

Eventually, it was revealed that there were three main suitors vying for TGH, including the executives of TGH itself, led by Tom Hansberger. Another was the Putnam Group of funds owned by the Marsh and McClennan Companies. The third was Franklin Resources.

John and Rosemary Galbraith were a highly successful husband and wife team in the investment world. Their company, Securities Fund Investors, provided marketing and sales support for TGH.

TEMPLETON, GALBRAITH AND HANSBERGER

(L-R): John Galbraith, Sir John Templeton, Tom Hansberger.

Although Templeton, Galbraith and Hansberger (TGH) did not officially become a company until 1986, the relationships that shaped the business had begun years earlier.

In 1954 John Templeton launched Templeton Growth Fund. In 1974 that fund had an international reputation when John Galbraith convinced Templeton to let him grow the business by improving marketing and distribution. He formed a separate company, Securities Fund Investors, Inc., to do so.

Templeton Investment Counsel, Inc., was created in Fort Lauderdale in 1979 under the leadership of Thomas Hansberger. This business provided research and analysis for the Templeton funds. In January 1986, these three businesses combined to form one company, which made an initial public offering of shares later that year.

For Franklin and Putnam, joining with Templeton was seen as a way for each to jump-start their presence in international equity investing.

Initially, Putnam seemed to have the inside track on the deal. After a flurry of meetings and phone calls, the conversation between Franklin and TGH suddenly stalled. Templeton's people wouldn't return phone calls. Even for insiders at TGH, John Templeton's legendary poker player's approach left people uncertain. "I remember coming back from a trip to Europe on a Friday night," says Marty Flanagan, "and Sir John said, 'Tomorrow morning you will meet your new owners.'" The meeting with Putnam's executives did not go well. There was strong resistance to a deal with Putnam among some of TGH's top executives. Templeton may have expected this, because he then turned to Franklin. For many years he had watched and invested in Franklin, and when the Putnam deal suddenly fell apart, the atmosphere surrounding the negotiations with Franklin quickly changed. Chuck was now allowed to talk to other members of the firm.

After due diligence revealed Templeton to be, in Chuck's words, a "lean, mean, fighting machine and clean as a whistle," it was time to begin the serious negotiations. Chuck Johnson spearheaded the talks, flying back and forth between California and the Bahamas and hosting Sir John in San Mateo. Dealing with Templeton was a challenge. While always courtly and even-tempered, Templeton was also an intimidating and demanding figure. One participant in the negotiations noted, "He grinds unbelievably fierce." He usually arrived for negotiations with only a lawyer and another executive or two to face Franklin's phalanx of executives and advisors. Chuck remembers watching Templeton, a severe stickler for details, sitting alone in a conference room reading through the thick merger contract, initialing and commenting on almost every page.

Templeton particularly objected to Franklin's continued inclusion of boilerplate language about "subject to financing" in the contract, while the company was making assurances that paying for the acquisition would present little difficulty. The offending language was eventually removed. The negotiations grew tense at times, but Templeton never raised his voice or appeared angry. The poker playing prowess he used to help pay his way through Yale was still well in evidence.

Templeton's attention to details tested the Franklin team. "Chuck's a very direct individual, hard charging and motivated," says Goldman's Berlinski. "Left to his own devices, he would prefer to get something done faster rather than slower." Charlie encouraged patience.

The critical element that allowed the merger to go through was Franklin's willingness to place the entire purchase price in escrow before the closing of the deal. Templeton was concerned that if the merger was made public, but then for some reason was not ultimately completed, it would severely impact the market value of TGH. To raise his comfort level, Templeton wanted the money "sitting there" in an escrow account where he could see it before signing on the dotted line. While the TGH team seeking to buy back the company had arranged the same amount of financing, only Franklin was able to convince its creditors to take the unusual risk of putting the funds in escrow prior to the close. Finally, at the end of July 1992, the announcement was made: The board of TGH had agreed to sell to Franklin Resources for the then-astonishing price of $913 million.

Wall Street pundits found new reason to admire Templeton when they learned of the deal, the largest mutual fund company merger in history. For Templeton, a man much concerned about both his historical legacy and the long-term interests of his 700,000 fund investors, the merger with Franklin Resources provided more than an enhancement to his retirement fund. He felt "the two organizations fit like a hand in a glove" with their contrasting equity and bond offerings. Perhaps more important, the merger allowed him to entrust his name and his professional legacy to a company he believed was well managed and shared many of his values and approaches to doing business. Franklin's longstanding emphasis on building strong relationships with networks of brokers who sold their funds was particularly important. Over the years, as no-load funds grew in popularity, both Franklin and Templeton regularly defended this intermediary model of mutual fund marketing as the best way to ensure that shareholders received the best possible service and earned the highest return from their assets by remaining long-term investors.

Templeton also shared with Franklin the belief that marketing is an equal partner in the success of any mutual fund company. Yet analysts

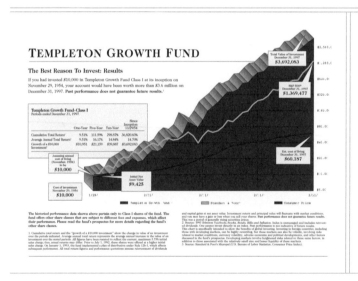

Templeton Growth Fund practically sold itself on its reputation for performance. For years, the primary sales tool for this fund was the well-known "mountain chart."

Sir John shakes hands with Chuck Johnson (left) and Greg Johnson (right) at the conclusion of Franklin's acquisition of TGH. As the Johnsons discovered, Templeton was a tough negotiator who meticulously reviewed hundreds of pages of documents on his own.

tended to view his funds as undermarketed. Peter Jones, who worked for Templeton as a wholesaler, hoped that now the sales organization would get some support. "Templeton was sold on reputation and track record," he says. Donald Reed, who joined Templeton in 1989 as portfolio manager and CEO of the Canadian operations, agreed. He remembered the only presentation used by his salespeople at that point was the famed Templeton "mountain chart" that depicted the growing value of an investment in Templeton Growth Fund from 1954 to the present. By merging with Franklin, Templeton placed his funds under the wings of one of the top sales organizations in the mutual fund industry.

The merger also gave John Templeton one additional bit of peace: "Now people will stop asking me, 'What's going to happen to my investment when John Templeton dies?'"

There was no question that Franklin paid a very generous price for TGH. Some analysts wondered about the wisdom of the merger,

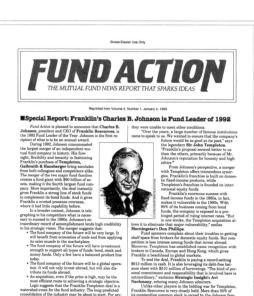

Charlie Johnson's leadership in the acquisition of Templeton, Galbraith and Hansberger earned him the "Fund Leader of the Year" award from *Fund Action* in 1992.

considering that Templeton's recent pre-merger performance was not quite as stellar as it had been in the past. The Johnsons, however, had few doubts about their decision. In one fell swoop, they had doubled the power of their brand, joining the image of Benjamin Franklin with that of Sir John Templeton, the master investor with the global grasp. They created the world's largest publicly traded mutual fund company, with over $89.9 billion under management. The combined firm now included a world-renowned international investing division and a transnational research infrastructure to support it. Furthermore, the two companies were, as Greg put it, "a perfect fit" since Franklin's fund offerings comprised about 80 percent fixed income funds and 13 percent equity funds, while Templeton provided the reverse, with 80 percent equity funds and 12 percent fixed income. Charlie's decision to acquire Templeton looked even more brilliant a year later when the combined company's net assets had grown to $107.5 billion. That year, Charlie was named Fund Leader of the Year by *Fund Action* for spearheading the largest merger of an independent mutual fund company in history.

INTEGRATING CULTURES

On the surface, the integration of two major mutual fund companies did not pose the same challenges that come from combining two large industrial operations. Franklin bought Templeton for its product line and the expertise that made that product attractive to customers. There were opportunities to realize efficiencies in the service operations, but the greater synergies came from being able to meet a broader range of investor needs. It was understood in the acquisition process that the Templeton investment team would be allowed, even encouraged, to keep doing what it did best— pick companies to invest in. Down the road, however, Franklin looked to create a single organization to handle sales and administration.

As Franklin's leadership looked at the challenges ahead, it also had to consider the unique history of the Templeton organization. For years, Templeton, Galbraith and Hansberger had been operated as a loose confederation of three organizations. John Templeton led the Research and Fund Management Team at the head office in Nassau. This work was supported by research offices around the globe, including the office led by Tom Hansberger in Fort Lauderdale, Florida. Meanwhile, Marketing, Administration and Shareholder Services were based in St. Petersburg, Florida, and led by John Galbraith.

The first step along the winding path to integration came in May 1993, when Charlie tapped Marty Flanagan to become Franklin's chief financial officer. Like the Johnsons, Flanagan had grown up in a world steeped in markets and investments. His grandfather and father had been commodities traders. As a boy he would sit on the floor of the Board of Trade with his father and watch as the bell rang and the screaming and yelling began. "Every day he was risking the family nest egg," Flanagan recalls of his father. What Flanagan took away from his mentorship at the dinner table was "to fully understand the risks involved in what you were doing, to understand the downside." In college in Texas, Flanagan pursued Ibero-American studies and accounting, earning a bachelor's degree in business administration. He spent time studying abroad in Madrid, Ecuador and Peru.

After graduating, he landed a job with Arthur Andersen in Dallas. His girlfriend, Jennifer (later his wife), had moved to Fort Lauderdale to work for a tiny firm, Templeton Investment Counsel, run by Hansberger. In November 1982, she persuaded Flanagan to come to Fort Lauderdale to a client conference hosted by Templeton. Flanagan was fascinated by the business, the clientele and the management—especially John Templeton. "It was the investment management culture that made the company attractive," Flanagan remembers. Over the next several months, he kept in touch with the group through Jennifer. Then one day Hansberger called to offer Flanagan a job managing the accounting side of the business. As Flanagan tells the story, "They hired me to keep Jennifer." In the meantime, in an unusual twist, Hansberger had married Jennifer's mother, so the family element was a strong force in the shaping of the business.

Despite his youth (23 at the time), Flanagan quickly became an important part of the small Templeton organization. Each week he spent two days in Nassau with John Templeton and three days in Fort Lauderdale with Hansberger and his investment team.

After he had been with the company just two years, Flanagan received an invitation from John Templeton to join him for lunch at the Lyford Cay Club one summer day. "I had never been invited back behind the pearly gates before," Flanagan remembers. Inside the club about a dozen investment bankers were gathered around a table. When Flanagan walked in, Templeton stood up and with a big smile said: "Everybody, this is Marty Flanagan. He is our expert on international reorganizations and initial public offerings, and he is going to be the one responsible for helping to take Templeton, Galbraith and Hansberger public." Flanagan was stunned. "Everybody around the table had to know I had no idea, none of that experience at all," he says, "but I was smart enough to remember the lesson all our dads teach us: Don't open your mouth in a room full of doubt. I sat down and smiled and listened."

Flanagan did indeed take TGH public in January 1986, and for the next six years he played an increasingly important role in managing the company's international expansion and global operations. During the negotiations for Franklin's acquisition of the company, he and Chuck spent a great deal of time together arguing and hammering out the details. By the time the deal was complete, they had developed a rapport that set the stage for the integration work ahead. Flanagan's move to San Mateo helped to cement the relationship and bridge the two organizations.

Some tensions inherent in the acquisition of Templeton did not ease. In the TGH culture, sales and marketing had always been kept very separate from investment management. When Jeff Everett joined the Fort Lauderdale office as a portfolio manager, he remembers, "You had these incredible mentors teaching you the business." Sales and marketing, remembers Marty Flanagan, "were expected to take care of themselves." Barely a year after the conclusion of the deal, Hansberger left the company to establish his own firm, Hansberger Global Investors, in Fort Lauderdale. Eventually, he recruited several former Templeton staffers to join him. For some of these employees, the opportunity to return to a smaller organization was attractive. For others, the desire for autonomy reflected in the pre-merger effort to orchestrate a management buyout was a major motivating factor.

Templeton offices
Fort Lauderdale,
Florida

   ⤷Chuck characterized the departures as a natural consequence of a bull market that created lots of opportunities for people with investment management experience. Overall, he said, the acquisition "has worked out very well." Indeed, by 1996 Templeton's open-end funds had grown to $34.4 billion. Most of Templeton's key portfolio managers, including Mark Mobius, Mark Holowesko and Gary Motyl, continued to be important players on Franklin Templeton's team.

SALES AND SERVICE IN ST. PETERSBURG

At the time of the acquisition, TGH employees in St. Petersburg, Florida, worried about whether they would have a job after the deal was done. Franklin had its own Shareholder Services Group based in San Mateo. With a recently opened new facility in Rancho Cordova, some employees imagined that Franklin would simply eliminate the Shareholder Services Group in St. Petersburg. Sales and marketing employees worried as well. "Every article written by the press focused on Franklin's strength in sales and distribution," remembers Peter Jones. People began to work on their resumes.

   ⤷Franklin quickly provided assurance that those resumes were unnecessary. Still remembering the effects of the Loma Prieta earthquake, Franklin executives recognized that with three service locations, the company's operations would be more secure. The Florida location also enabled Franklin Templeton to provide more timely shareholder services to customers on the East Coast. On the sales side, Franklin saw the underdeveloped potential of the Templeton brand name. As senior vice president and assistant national sales manager in 1992, Greg was assigned to align the pricing structures and integrate the distribution systems of the two firms. He made sure the team in St. Petersburg knew they had a bright future in the Franklin organization.

Without a doubt, Templeton's marketing and sales organizations needed development and support. Until the late 1980s, the company had not had a wholesale network. "A financial advisor had to discover the company," says Peter Jones. When Jones came to TGH in 1989, he was one of the company's first wholesalers, with responsibility for seven southeastern states. "We had a huge advantage because of the name," Jones says, but Templeton's reputation for frugality created its own challenges. Management tightly controlled the amount of sales literature wholesalers could use. "I had to make friends in the mailroom and sometimes sneak literature out the back door." Wholesalers had no budget to share the costs of a client seminar and none of the usual coffee mugs, T-shirts and pens to leave as a reminder for the brokers. Overall, it was a tough environment for a salesperson.

Franklin immediately began to provide more support for the Templeton products, but for most of 1993, the organization continued to operate with a great deal of autonomy. The real work of integrating the wholesaling team and the product line with Franklin began when Greg became president of Franklin Templeton Distributors in 1994.

Another major decision that had to be made after the Franklin Templeton merger was how, and if, the combined companies should harmonize the fee structure of their various funds. This required counterbalancing the desire to preserve Templeton's unique corporate culture with the need to earn a suitable return on the funds. It also meant finding a way to please brokers who wanted both an attractive commission and lower upfront loads to facilitate fund marketing.

TGH historically had an upfront sales charge of 8.75 percent, while Franklin had a 4 percent sales charge on its funds. But under pressure from the market, where the trend was clearly toward lowering upfront fees, TGH lowered the sales charge on its funds to 5.75 percent and added a 12b-1 fee shortly before the merger. While this rate was still higher than Franklin's front-end sales charge, the newly merged companies decided not to standardize fees companywide. Summarizing the array of fee changes at Templeton in Canada, Don Reed of Templeton Management, Ltd., in Toronto, said they were "inevitable" in the current marketplace and noted that 84 percent of shareholders voted to approve the new policies.

Franklin enjoyed favorable press for its resistance to the increasingly widespread 12b-1 fees, but faced growing criticism for levying a 4 percent commission on reinvested dividends, which it divided half and half with brokers. In response, in 1994 Franklin "conceded a point," in the words of one analyst, and submitted to shareholders a proposal to end the commission on reinvested dividends; impose a modest 12b-1 fee of .05 percent to .25 percent; and raise the front-end load to 4.25 percent on fixed income funds and 4.5 percent on equity funds. The proposal,

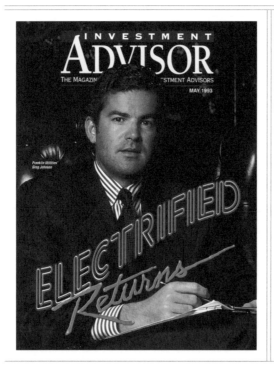

The continued success of Franklin Utilities Fund put Greg Johnson on the cover of *Investment Advisor* magazine in May 1993. Managed by Greg and his father, Charlie, Franklin Utilities Fund was among the top 12 best-performing, open-end mutual funds from March 1983 to March 1993.

which according to a company spokesperson was devised "to bring our pricing in line with the industry," was quickly approved.

⮜ While Franklin decided that certain fee policy changes made sense in the current marketplace, it continued until 1995 to oppose another major industry trend: the introduction of multiple share classes. Multiple share classes, commonly known as A, B and C shares, did not actually eliminate broker commissions, but instead reallocated them in ways that investors found more appealing. Franklin believed in the classic business model of distributing funds through intermediaries like brokers, who then received their compensation from a straightforward, upfront sales fee. Greg Johnson, vice president of marketing in 1993, echoed his father Charlie's long-standing sentiments about different class shares, but by 1994 Greg conceded that the growing popularity of B shares was hurting Franklin's sales as its front-loaded funds became harder to sell.

⮜ Unable to resist the force of the market, Franklin developed its own approach in 1995, launching two share classes. Class I shares reflected the long tradition of a front-end sales charge. Class II shares included a smaller (1 percent) front-end sales charge, but compensated with higher annual fees plus an additional 1 percent back-end charge for shares liquidated within 18 months of purchase. As Greg told a reporter about this decision, "We've been hesitant about bringing out multiple class structures, but this recognizes a growing trend."

⮜ The establishment of two classes of shares still left unresolved one competitive threat Franklin faced from the fund pricing innovations of the 1990s. B shares continued to grow in popularity, particularly within the bank sales channel. With deregulation, banks were eager to position themselves more broadly as financial service providers, and fund companies saw an opportunity to assist banks in this process by helping them offer mutual fund products to their customers. Franklin had established a sales division dedicated to banks in 1992. Four years later, however, it was apparent that getting banks to sell funds was not as straightforward as originally hoped. As Greg later put it, "We are no longer as blindly

Reason #16 to consider working with an investment professional.

A Professional's Financial Game Plan

A gifted individual like Joe Montana knows his true expertise is on the playing field, not in the financial field. He relies on investment professionals to develop a workable game plan for his family and his future.

An investment professional can offer experience, training, perspective and focus to guide you through thousands of options in today's domestic and international investment arena.

Franklin Templeton has always believed you can benefit from professional advice to help in asset allocation, investment suitability, diversification, and service.

Call your investment professional today.

This ad is a paid endorsement. Use of an investment professional cannot assure your financial goals will be met. The testimonial used may not be representative of the experience of all customers.

Sponsored by Franklin Templeton Distributors, Inc.

FRANKLIN TEMPLETON

Franklin Templeton Distributors, Inc., 777 Mariners Island Blvd., San Mateo, CA 94404   KIP94

FRANKLIN INCREASINGLY BECAME KNOWN FOR ITS ADVERTISING AT THE BEGINNING OF THE 1990S. IN 1991, AFTER GREG BECAME ASSISTANT NATIONAL SALES MANAGER, HE NEGOTIATED AN AGREEMENT WITH JOE MONTANA TO BE A NATIONAL SPOKESPERSON FOR FRANKLIN. AS QUARTERBACK OF THE SAN FRANCISCO 49ERS IN THE MID-1980S, MONTANA HAD LED HIS TEAM TO THREE SUPER BOWL CHAMPIONSHIPS.

optimistic as we were." In the early 1990s, when bond funds were still highly popular, Franklin enjoyed a number one ranking in bank sales. Subsequently Franklin's sales through banks declined steadily, from $4 billion in 1993 to $1.8 billion in 1995. By the mid-1990s, Franklin had fallen to second behind Putnam.

There were several reasons for this decline. As the Internet boom began to take off and investors started to embrace stock funds, Franklin was still largely associated with fixed income products. Consumers were not fully aware of the company's newly strengthened presence in equity investing after the merger with Templeton. Finally, as Greg noted at the time, Franklin's dual share class option was not sufficiently appealing to the bank market. B shares, with their absence of any front-end sales charge, accounted for the majority of bank sales. "We will not be where we should be in the bank channel until we have B shares available," he emphasized. "It's just too strong a pricing force through that distribution channel, and I think it cost us a lot in sales."

ACQUIRING MUTUAL SERIES

The Templeton acquisition had given Franklin a strong portfolio of international equity funds, but the company still needed a broader line of domestic equity products. In 1996 Franklin began looking at another major acquisition. Mutual Series was well recognized for its strength in domestic equity investing. The firm had four major funds in 1996: Mutual Beacon, Mutual Discovery, Mutual Qualified and Mutual Shares. Each of them had five-star ratings from Morningstar. The company was also on the threshold of launching a new international fund called Mutual European Fund. With total assets under management of roughly $17 billion, Mutual Series was a prize for any potential buyer.

Mutual had been created in 1949 by several men, including Max Heine, who managed investments for themselves and their friends. A German Jewish refugee, Heine had grown the fund's assets under management to about $5 million by 1975. That year, Heine hired a young

MAX HEINE

Max Heine used to say his strategy was "to buy a dollar for 50 cents." In the sick room of capitalism, he looked for firms that might once again be restored to health. His strategy paid off. After an initial investment in Mutual Shares of $25,000 in 1949, the value of his untouched portfolio rose to $1.8 million by 1987.

Heine's protégé, Michael Price, showed a similar enthusiasm for troubled stocks, and he assembled a team of portfolio managers who made Mutual Series a star performer. After Franklin Templeton acquired Mutual Series in 1996, this team added an important new approach to the range of options available to Franklin Templeton clients—value investing.

college graduate named Michael Price, who became his protégé. When Heine was struck and killed by a car in Arizona at the age of 78, Price became the sole owner of the company at age 37. Under a deal that he and Heine had worked out years earlier, Price paid Heine's heirs $4 million for the business. Shortly thereafter, the firm moved from Manhattan to Short Hills, New Jersey, a location closer to his home. Price did not, however, change the strategy. "We were a buyer of undervalued stocks," he says. "You do your homework. If you do the work and wait for the market to hand you a stock on the cheap, you'll come out all right."

As an investor, Price developed a reputation over the next several years as a "stalker of underperforming CEOs" and an important dealmaker. Price was credited, for example, with bringing Chase Manhattan and Chemical Bank together, an arrangement that led to the $10 billion merger of the two major banks. Some people compared Price to the corporate raiders of the 1980s like T. Boone Pickens, Carl Icahn or Jimmy Goldsmith. But as *Fortune* observed, Price wasn't investing just for himself. He was a mutual fund manager, and assets he invested came from "small shareholders across the country. In other words, this is a raider with whom you and I can go along for the ride." Price also looked at whatever deals he made for the long run as a value investor.

When word got out on the Street in January 1996 that Price was interested in selling, some speculated that it was because he felt the market was overvalued and feared a fall. For Price, however, the decision was personal. He was ready for a change. Price reportedly had conversations with several potential buyers, including PIMCO Advisors, LP, First Union Corp. and New England Investment Cos. Franklin at first was not interested. As Chuck later told *Fortune,* "You have to ask yourself why you're buying something when the smartest man on Wall Street is selling it." But after looking more closely at the potential synergies, the Franklin team changed its mind.

The deal between Franklin Templeton and Heine Securities was announced on June 25, 1996. Under the terms of the agreement, Price would receive $550 million in cash and another 1.1 million shares of Franklin Resources. Price would have to hold onto the stock for two years, and would initially invest $150 million of the cash proceeds in Mutual Series' funds with a minimum balance of $100 million for five years. Charlie told the press that the deal was

MICHAEL PRICE

Max Heine tested Michael Price the day he walked in the door. "So what do you like?" the older man asked. A student of Wall Street fresh out of college, Price told Heine about a merger that was in the news. On the strength of Price's analysis, Heine picked up the phone and bought 20,000 shares.

Twenty-three years old, Price had grown up on Long Island in Roslyn, New York. His father was a graduate of the famous Wharton School of Business in Philadelphia. Price didn't have the grades to follow his father to Wharton or get into an Ivy League school. Instead, he went to the University of Oklahoma "because I loved football."

After graduation, Price's father arranged for the interview with Heine. It was the beginning of an unusual and successful partnership in which Heine taught Price "about valuation."

By the mid-1980s, Price had developed a reputation for finding value in troubled companies and pressing management to unlock that value for shareholders. For this he was both feared and respected.

great for both entities. The Mutual Series portfolio of products would give Franklin a strong hand in domestic equity investing.

⁐Some analysts reacted strongly to what they called the "eye-popping" price Franklin had agreed to. The deal reflected a substantial premium—6.8 times Mutual's estimated revenues. Chuck Johnson felt that was the wrong way to look at the deal. "Our whole focus was on the price to EBITDA (earnings before interest, taxes, depreciation and amortization). This ratio was very reasonable." In any case, after the success of the Templeton acquisition, few analysts were willing to be too critical of Franklin's strategy.

ALIGNING THE SERVICE OPERATIONS

At the time of the Templeton acquisition, Franklin executives considered the idea of integrating the technology systems that supported shareholder services and the transfer agency. Templeton had been using a product from SunGard, the same vendor that supplied Franklin, but shortly before the sale it switched to a proprietary system called Titan, which ran on an IBM mainframe in the St. Petersburg data center. After evaluating the prospects for consolidating the systems, Franklin's management decided that at least for the short run, running parallel systems made more sense.

⁐With the acquisition of Mutual Series, the idea of running parallel systems threatened to deteriorate into chaos. According to Frank Isola, "We were operating off three separate shareholder accounting systems and attempting to make it appear transparent to the customer. Needless to say, our problems were many, and transparent it was not."

⁐Late in 1996, Franklin decided to consolidate its records onto one platform: Investar One from SunGard. To accomplish this task, Isola, working with Nancy Hessel and others, had to transfer records from three different systems. The project was to take place in three phases. If successful, it would be the largest project of its kind ever undertaken in the mutual fund industry. In March 1997, Isola optimistically expected the project to be completed by the end of the year. SunGard worked hard to facilitate the transition, motivated by the fact that both Franklin and Mutual were already using SunGard (although different software) and the prospect that Templeton would now become a user as well. The challenges were numerous and complex. Investar had to be scaled to handle the tremendous volume of Franklin Templeton transactions. At the beginning of 1998, it had to track 121 different funds, more than five million accounts and assets valued at roughly $178 billion.

By the fall of 1998, Franklin's cutover to the new Investar system was complete. But this system integration affected only Franklin, Templeton and Mutual customers in the United States. At the same time this transition was underway, Franklin also had to wrestle with fundamental changes caused by the rise of the Internet.

By the late 1990s, it was clear that the pace of change had significantly quickened at Franklin. Franklin had entered the 1990s with $45.1 billion in net assets under management. By the fall of 1997, following the acquisitions of two large mutual fund businesses, the company, now branded as Franklin Templeton, had net assets under management of $226 billion. It had also revamped its pricing structure and integrated a new technology platform. Now business was booming overseas, and the company quickly had to respond to new challenges, new investors and the emergence of a fast-moving global market.

ACQUISITIONS FUEL GROWTH
FRANKLIN'S ASSETS UNDER MANAGEMENT (IN BILLIONS), 1988–1997

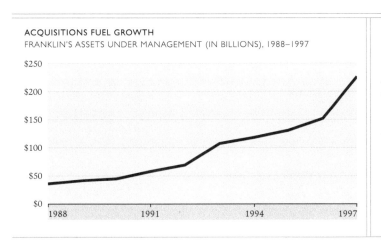

As Franklin Templeton expanded into new markets, assets under management (AUM) continued to grow. Between 1988 and 1997, AUM increased nearly 500 percent.

CHAPTER V

History Repeats
On a Global Stage

Shown here by a Templeton advertisement, Murray Simpson arrived in Hong Kong in 1994 to lead Franklin Templeton's expansion in Asia. Fueled by a growing middle class, the mutual fund industry was poised for rapid international growth.

Opposite: Street scene in Varanasi, India, one of the oldest continually inhabited cities in the world and the location of a Franklin Templeton office.

History Repeats
On a Global Stage

Take time for all things;
great haste makes great waste.

— BENJAMIN FRANKLIN

Charlie Johnson understood that the history of mutual funds in the United States was likely to be repeated on the world stage, spurred by increasingly integrated financial markets, growing world trade and a rising middle class in Europe, Asia and Latin America. By the mid-1990s, the Franklin Templeton team felt the time was right to expand its wholesaling and retail presence in these markets.

Franklin Templeton's international growth was driven by a comprehensive, two-tiered global strategy. First, the company watched for

Shortly after opening an office in Edinburgh in 1988, TGH launched its first open-end mutual funds targeting the UK market. From Edinburgh, the company began its European expansion.

122

and took advantage of new opportunities that arose from economic reforms worldwide. Then, once it decided to expand into a new region, it followed a "think global, act local" approach to building the business.

Charlie succinctly described the first part of this global strategy to *Global Investor* magazine in 1997: "I see the world as an opportunity as political barriers to investing come down in different countries." This view was rooted in his belief that parallels to the patterns and cycles that had occurred in the U.S. fund industry during the past 40 years were developing internationally. As he told a reporter, when he began his career in the mid-1950s, mutual funds were relatively obscure, and banks and insurance companies were the main vehicles people used to grow their savings. Charlie pointed to South Africa, where insurance companies were the most popular savings institution, as one example of a country where the investment style remained similar to post–World War II America. Just as mutual funds became the dominant savings vehicle in the United States, he predicted, "I think you will find that over the next 40 years that will be true worldwide."

The "think global, act local" component of Franklin Templeton's global strategy meant that wherever it expanded, the company sought to promote the same principles that had guided it since the 1950s: excellent service, support for wholesalers and intermediaries, investor education and diverse products backed by a code of integrity. Franklin Templeton wanted local partners who shared these values and who could also provide insight into local investor preferences. The company would find that the international learning curve was steep, and patience would be needed.

EXPANDING IN EUROPE

Franklin Templeton's move into Europe was built upon the pre-merger efforts of John Templeton's firm to establish a presence in the region. Templeton's famed Growth Fund was first sold in Europe to United States servicemen stationed in Germany, but it was not until 1988 that Templeton International made a concentrated move into what it saw as the untapped potential of the European market. The company began by establishing a subsidiary, Templeton Unit Trust Managers, in Edinburgh, Scotland, and later that year launched two funds directed to European investors, Global Growth Fund and Global Balanced Fund. The former was designed to be a mirror image of Templeton Growth Fund.

The European market was difficult to enter as an outsider, since each country had different regulations, tax laws and cultural attitudes toward investing. Governments also sought to protect and promote their domestic financial enterprises and were not welcoming to foreign firms. The distribution networks also varied. In Germany, France and Spain, for example, fund distribution was concentrated among banks. In the United Kingdom it was dominated by independent financial advisors (IFAs). In Italy it was split between banks and independent advisors.

This fractured market began to change with the formation of the European Union (EU) and its efforts to devise standardized, Europe-wide regulations on everything from safety standards for kitchen appliances to financial services. The adoption of the euro by 11 countries in 1999 marked the true launch of an integrated market. For the mutual fund industry, the march to a more open and unified Europe began a decade earlier, in October 1989, when the European Union instituted new rules regulating mutual funds. Under these new rules, any funds that obtained the proper designation could be freely marketed to any country within the European Union. The one caveat to this new cross-border free market was that a "home country regulation, host country marketing" formula had to be followed, which meant every fund manager had to abide by the different marketing regulations of each country in which it sought to sell shares. After the new fund regulations were established, financial management companies worked quickly to launch investment funds that conformed to the new criteria.

Despite the EU's efforts to establish a Europe-wide, cross-border fund market, the continued strength of local norms or standards in the fund industry was evident. Each country used different names and terms for these mutual funds. France and Luxembourg, the first countries to create these new funds, created the SICAV or *Société d'Investissement à Capital Variable.* In the United Kingdom, where the "unit trust" long dominated the fund market, the OEIC (Open-Ended Investment Company) was authorized in 1996 to conform to EU rules. In Italy, they were called the FCI for *fondi comune di investimento*; in Spain, the *fondos de inversión mobiliaria* or FIM; in Germany, *investmentfonds*. Overall, SICAVs became the most widely used and recognized type of fund across Europe, largely because the majority of fund companies chose to launch SICAVs from a domicile in Luxembourg due to that country's more relaxed regulations and lower tax rates.

⟡In these years, Marty Flanagan spent a great deal of time traveling through Europe and Asia. He helped open Templeton's unit trust business in Edinburgh and launched offices in Hong Kong and Singapore. "This was the formative stage of putting early seeds in the ground," he says. Templeton established its own domicile in Luxembourg in 1990–91 and launched a growing number of SICAVs for the European market under the Global Strategy Funds umbrella. To facilitate the marketing of its Luxembourg-based funds, Templeton also established offices in Germany and Switzerland. In Germany, Templeton Growth Fund had been sold for many years by Joe Becker, a local wholesaler. Flanagan worked with Becker to internalize the German sales operation to the Templeton organization. The company also worked to make its new SICAVs attractive to the UK market by initially offering special incentives to IFAs to market them to their clients. The persistent "Europhobia" of both the UK government and IFAs, however, stymied most attempts to market the company's SICAVs within Britain, a problem that would continue after the merger with Franklin Resources.

⟡Charlie was pleased by the extent of Templeton's business in Europe in 1992. "It was one of the few American funds that was registered in Germany," he says, "and they had about $500 to $600 million in assets." Franklin Templeton built upon TGH's foundation by opening more offices in Europe, expanding the Luxembourg-registered SICAV line of

Global Strategy Funds, and marketing these funds to a steadily growing number of EU countries. But it was tough going. When Hans Wisser took over the German office in 1995, for example, it had about $500 million under management. All of the business came from IFAs, but the IFAs handled just a small share of the mutual fund industry in Germany. "Banks had their own proprietary funds," says Wisser, "and we had no chance to take them head-on."

⟜ The cornerstone of Franklin Templeton's European strategy was to negotiate agreements with key banks in different countries and to convince them of the value of offering third-party fund products. Like U.S. banks in the 1950s, European banks were historically resistant to offering third-party funds, but as equity funds grew more popular, banks started to realize the value of selling these funds as a way to bring in customers for their banking services. The trend toward this "open architecture" accelerated after Citibank entered the German market in 1999 and began offering third-party funds to private clients. "That inspired and put pressure on other banks," says Wisser.

⟜ The opening of the marketplace rewarded companies like Franklin Templeton that had spent years building relationships. In 1998

Sir John Templeton registered Templeton Growth Fund in Germany in 1981, and by 1995 assets under management had grown to approximately $500 million. Shown here: Franklin Templeton's first office in Frankfurt.

the assets under management for Templeton's Luxembourg funds grew 121 percent, the highest percentage increase of any European fund company. By 2000 Franklin Templeton became the eighth-largest mutual fund company in Germany.

One sign of Franklin Templeton's growing confidence and presence in Europe was the decision in May 2000 to rename and reorganize its SICAV range of funds. The Templeton Global Strategy Funds were replaced by a more comprehensive product known as the Franklin Templeton Investment Funds. No longer did the company feel a need to rely solely upon the Templeton brand as an entrée into the European market. The new Franklin Templeton Investment Funds umbrella provided something for everyone for European investors, including the global bargain-hunting approach of Templeton funds, the fixed income and growth equity management of Franklin funds, and the deep value investing of Mutual Series.

While Franklin enjoyed increasing success in much of Europe during the 1990s, the company struggled in the United Kingdom. In part this was due to Britain's continued reluctance to embrace the EU's direction. As one spokesperson put it, the company grew "frustrated by the slowness of the UK authorities in allowing investment products to be priced, packaged and taxed in a way that is more appealing to foreign as well as to domestic investors." When the United Kingdom finally issued regulations that allowed the establishment of more EU-friendly funds in 1996, Franklin applauded the move. Franklin had also learned that attracting the support of IFAs highlighted the continuing need to "act local" by marketing the right fund products for each market.

BUILDING ON THE BASE IN EAST ASIA

As the Taiwan business began to take off in the early 1990s, Chuck Johnson, the head of Franklin's international operations, decided the time was right to move into other areas of East Asia. To help spearhead this expansion, he called upon Murray Simpson, Franklin's longtime outside counsel, to open an office in Hong Kong in 1994. Following the "highlight

MURRAY SIMPSON

When Chuck Johnson called in 1994, Murray Simpson was pleasantly surprised. "Would you like to go to Hong Kong?" Chuck asked. "Sure," Simpson replied, thinking that Chuck had some short adventure in mind.

A longtime legal advisor to Franklin Resources, Simpson had helped Franklin go public in 1971 and had served as outside general counsel for decades. He had watched Charlie's children grow up. Over the years, there had been other trips with the family. But Chuck had something else in mind.

"No, no," he said. "I mean do you want to go to Hong Kong?" Chuck wanted Simpson to move to Hong Kong to lead the expansion of Franklin Templeton's retail business in Asia. Intrigued by the opportunity, Simpson agreed to take the job.

Arriving in Hong Kong in September 1994, he stayed for six years, opening additional offices in Singapore, South Korea and Japan and establishing the foundation for the growth of Franklin Templeton's other Far Eastern operations.

Templeton first" strategy, the Hong Kong division was called Templeton Franklin Investment Services (Asia). Slated to stay for three years, Simpson extended his stay in Hong Kong. "Unlike the United States, where you can walk in and say, 'Yes, I'm Franklin Templeton, we're a big investor,' in Asia it doesn't mean anything," he says. "You have to be there. You have to show your face, and it takes time. It's not just reputation, it's getting investors and distributors comfortable with you and developing a level of trust and confidence in your company."

There was evidence by 1996 that Hong Kong investors were becoming comfortable with Franklin. Market share grew, and volume increased each month. Simpson stayed in Asia long enough to become a prominent figure in the Hong Kong investment community and take Franklin Templeton into Singapore, Korea and Japan. The company launched its first fund sold directly to the Singapore market in June 1996. This was an emerging markets fund, the first fund of its type available for sale in the country. Four other funds soon followed, and Franklin Templeton became the first company to offer Singapore investors a way to easily switch money between an array of funds. By July 1996, the fund had attracted approximately $40 million (Singapore dollars) in assets. Simpson was also heartened to see that the majority of the investors in the fund were "first-time investors," because "one of our goals was to educate the public about investment in our funds."

The organization and management of the Singapore umbrella funds demonstrated how Franklin worked to form close connections between its various operations as it expanded. As Marty Flanagan describes it, the strength of Franklin Templeton in Germany, Singapore and elsewhere around the world started with the early seeds Templeton placed in foreign markets before the merger and then continued in the early 1990s with the Luxembourg-based SICAVs. By the late 1990s, the SICAVs became "the tentacles into some of these other markets around the world, and have now been so successful for the organization." The Singapore funds, for example, were actually components of the Luxembourg-registered Templeton Global Strategy SICAV.

Based in this building in Hong Kong, Franklin Templeton's Asian team helped the company expand into Singapore, South Korea and Japan in the 1990s.

The same year Franklin began selling funds in Singapore, it also made a move into Korea, where government policies were opening up the country's economy and enabling joint ventures between local companies and foreign enterprises. In the summer of 1996, Templeton Franklin Investment Services (Asia) signed a joint venture with Ssangyong Investment and Securities Co., Ltd., "to create and locally register new mutual funds in Korea." Franklin became only the second foreign fund company to open operations in what was then the ninth-largest mutual fund market in the world. In Korea, as in other emerging markets, enormous opportunity did not equate with immediate success. The fund industry was dominated by eight companies, three national and five regional, which together controlled over 70 percent of the fund assets under management. Even so, according to *The Asian Wall Street Journal*, Franklin offered what many small investors wanted. After telling a reporter about her fear of investing in the stock market herself, one Korean investor said, "Then I heard about foreign mutual funds coming into the market. I heard that they distribute risk and that they can invest worldwide. I need something secure like that.... I'm willing to pay the

Charlie and Ann Johnson with Vijay and Swati Advani in front of the Taj Mahal in Agra in June 1998.
A rising middle class in India created new opportunities for Franklin Templeton in Southeast Asia.

management fee these companies charge if the fund is managed correctly and they give me long-term security." Her choice when investing her savings was a Templeton mutual fund.

⌐Franklin also entered into a joint venture in 1997 with Sumitomo Life Insurance, Japan's third-largest life insurance company. Under this deal, Franklin provided Sumitomo with advice on equity investing outside Japan, while Sumitomo, in return, made a significant investment in the Templeton Global Strategy Funds based in Luxembourg. Charlie was convinced that in emerging markets "a lot of development in the industry will be local with many companies setting up joint ventures." He believed this was the best way to quickly acquire local knowledge of market conditions, regulations and business relationships.

INVESTING IN INDIA

Vijay Advani knew the markets of many countries around the globe. In 1995 he flew from Washington, D.C., to Fort Lauderdale to meet Chuck Johnson. Raised in Bombay (renamed Mumbai in 1995), the son of the chief financial officer of a large Indian steel company, Advani had come to the United States to earn an M.B.A. at the University of Massachusetts at Amherst. After graduate school, he joined the International Finance Corporation (IFC), a part of the World Bank Group. At the IFC, he worked on a variety of projects in emerging markets in Africa, the Middle East, eastern Europe and Russia. In the late 1980s, he went to Sri Lanka to help engineer financial reforms, and while working to establish the framework for the country's mutual fund industry, he met Mark Mobius, Greg McGowan and others from the Templeton organization. "We developed a strong personal relationship," he remembers, "and brought Templeton in as a minority stakeholder in the first mutual fund in Sri Lanka." Years later, when Advani was ready to leave the IFC and the World Bank, McGowan convinced him to talk to Franklin.

⌐The conversation between Advani and Chuck was reserved at first. "We talked about Russia, Poland and India," Advani remembers. "He was like a sponge, wanting to know all my experiences." Chuck wanted to hire

Advani to go back to India to help Franklin open a business, but Advani was not interested. He was intent on working in eastern Europe. "We went back and forth," Advani says. In the end, he could not resist Chuck's persuasive energy. In June 1995, he left his family in Washington, D.C., flew to India and took up residence at the Oberoi Hotel in Mumbai where "every waiter and concierge became my family." For the next three months, he focused on launching Franklin's retail business in India.

At the time, most observers felt there was little prospect for success in India. With a government that favored socialistic solutions and a population that tended to be anti-foreign, India seemed an unlikely place to launch a global investment company. The majority of the citizens in this largely agrarian country were low-income farmers who tended to invest their limited savings in land, gold and jewelry. Stock and fund investors were still a very small percentage of India's population of more than one billion. Among those who had invested in stocks, the collapse of a market bubble in India in the early 1990s had resulted in a great deal of anger and investor complaints to regulators. Many thought India's new private fund industry was dead before it even got started.

Advani's work, however, was aided by the fact that India was a relatively free and democratic society. A diverse private sector of countless small- and medium-sized businesses played a vital role in India's commercial life. New enterprises were arising to take advantage of India's expanding global connections, huge educated workforce and lower wages. Around the time that Franklin Templeton developed serious interest in the country, India already had 20 million fund shareholders, and the middle class was growing and seeking new ways to invest. The culture of saving in India was also very strong.

Advani, like Charlie and Chuck, recognized that the privatization of the fund industry in India represented a huge opportunity. After arriving in Mumbai, he secured a license and formed Franklin Templeton Asset Management (India) with an Indian investment company called Hathway Investments. Franklin owned 75 percent of the operation.

The partnership hoped to launch Templeton India Growth Fund. Advani and Mobius visited 21 cities in India to raise money. At the end of the roadshow, however, they had raised only $2 million to $3 million. "The regulator required us to have $10.7 million," Advani says. "I was paranoid they would shut us down." So Advani and his team started working the phones, calling everyone they knew, and soon raised the additional cash.

As they worked to market the new fund, the Franklin Templeton team faced a widespread lack of understanding of the nature of mutual funds, born partly from the years of government-guaranteed gains before privatization. Brokers were blamed for many of the industry's ills because they commonly promoted funds as a way to make quick stock market gains while also convincing new investors they were as safe as bank savings accounts. "You had people handing out fliers for funds on street corners," Advani remembers. What was needed to grow India's fund industry was a program of comprehensive investor education. As always, Franklin Templeton took the high road, working to educate brokers and investors through its own advertising campaigns, seminars and training programs.

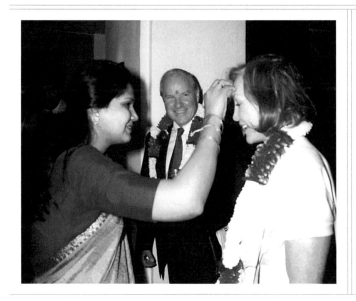

In June 1998, Ann Johnson received a traditional Indian welcome of an *aarti* and a *tilak* from Jigisha Bhayani of Fixed Income, as Charlie Johnson watched.

As president of Franklin Templeton International, Chuck gave Advani a good deal of freedom in setting up the business. As in Taiwan, it was not easy at first. Many questioned Franklin's decision to move into India. Jenny (Johnson) Bolt recalls consultants from McKinsey commenting, "I don't know why you guys are in India. That will take a long time to turn around." But Charlie remained optimistic, declaring in 1997 that "India will be a good market if and when regulations are improved.... More and more of the bureaucratic barriers and red tape are coming down."

Charlie witnessed the changes taking place in India on his first visit to Franklin Templeton's offices, and he also made an impression on the staff. "That was the first time people in our office saw how humble he is," says Advani, "despite all that he has accomplished. He took time with each person. He told them what they were doing reminded him of his work to build Franklin 30 years earlier." The staff in India also invigorated Charlie, giving him an even stronger sense of how the past would repeat itself in India and other emerging markets around the world.

SECURING BUSINESS IN SOUTH AMERICA

For years Franklin had wanted to expand its business to South America, but the timing was never right, so the company's presence was limited to a dealer who sold Franklin's funds. In the 1990s, however, Franklin Templeton began a careful expansion into South America by marketing its funds in Argentina and Brazil. These countries had been characterized by repressive military governments, flashes of violent revolution, tightly controlled economies, high rates of poverty, illiquid stock markets and often staggering inflation. But with the return of civilian governments to Argentina and Brazil, things began to change. In Argentina, President Carlos Menem, elected in 1988, promoted privatizing government enterprises, opening the economy to foreign investment, and stabilizing the Argentine currency by tying it to the U.S. dollar. President Fernando Cardoso in Brazil orchestrated similar reforms starting in the mid-1990s. These government-led reforms paralleled another trend in the region: the privatization of pension funds. Pension reform put the responsibility for managing retirement saving and investing in the hands of individuals.

⌐The adoption of the North American Free Trade Agreement (NAFTA) in 1994 also fueled economic growth and entrepreneurship in South America. "It led to the rise of a middle class in Mexico, Argentina and Chile," Advani explains, "which created excellent opportunities for Franklin Templeton." Franklin Templeton executives were well aware of the risks of operating in South America. While excess regulation was often a stumbling block in Europe, the lack of strong enforcement of economic regulations in South America led to what Jed Plafker, executive managing director at Franklin Templeton, called "wild times." As a young legal counsel in the mid-1990s, Plafker traveled to South America to discuss a shareholders' rights dispute with the CEO of a department store chain. Arriving at the company headquarters, he soon found himself surrounded by imposing bodyguards with automatic weapons. But gun-toting executives by no means represented the majority of local investors in the region, and through a gradual and focused approach, Franklin worked to build its presence in South America.

⌐In Argentina, Franklin Templeton opened its first office in the mid-1990s during a period one reporter called "a window of opportunity for mutual fund companies to team up with local banks and brokerage firms." The office was used as a base for equity research and for marketing to institutions and pension funds. For a variety of reasons, Franklin was more cautious about entering the retail market in Argentina. There were a limited number of liquid stocks available for investing locally, and laws restricting saving or investing capital abroad were still in place. The history of market instability and high inflation rates also made the small pool of potential retail investors highly risk averse.

⌐But as capital markets continued to develop in the region, Franklin was convinced that a growing number of investors were becoming interested in finding safe ways to invest in both local and foreign equities. The company tested this belief in 1997 by expanding into Brazil while the São Paulo Stock Exchange was booming (it was up over 70 percent by August of that year). When announcing the move into Brazil, Franklin clearly indicated the "act local" component of its global expansion strategy. As Greg explained, "We don't go in with a cookie-cutter approach.... You have to understand the local environment and determine how we can best position ourselves in those countries in terms of strategy, product development, target market, global products and international products." For more sophisticated investors in Latin America who were already aware of the international fund marketplace, Franklin Templeton funds were made available starting in 1997 on the Internet, via Charles Schwab's offshore fund supermarket service, the Mutual Fund Trading Center.

RUSSIAN REALITIES

With the beginning of the new millennium, Franklin Templeton's patient strategy for global expansion began to reap rewards. Efforts by Chuck Johnson and others to establish offices around the globe and nurture local relationships began to pay off handsomely as barriers to competition were removed. But success didn't come in every market.

⇔In many parts of the world, the transition to orderly and formal capital markets took time. Getting in on the ground floor of these developing markets was critical, but also demanded keen judgment and an intuitive sense of the local culture. Russia was a case in point. Following the collapse and breakup of the Soviet Union in 1991, the new Russian Federation instituted a rapid and comprehensive process of privatization. By 1997 it appeared that Russia had successfully shed the burden of a depressed state-controlled economy and was enjoying a growing free market system. Russia's GDP, after falling steadily from 1989 through 1996, registered slight growth between 1996 and 1997. The country also began to experience a stock boom. The market rose 156 percent in 1996.

⇔The Russian government began to offer licenses to foreign mutual fund companies in 1996, and Templeton Worldwide made plans to move into the country. "There's no reason why we can't duplicate in Russia what we have in the United States," said Mark Mobius in March 1997. By then, Franklin Templeton had established a joint venture with a Russian firm named Aton and secured a license to market funds under the company name of CJSC Templeton. Templeton launched its first fund for the Russian market in late 1997. As Sam Forester of Templeton Worldwide explained, "We're happy to start off slowly in these countries [like India and Russia]. We'd rather wait and get it right. You can't turn on the light switch the first day you raise the money." Other early arrivals in the promising mutual fund industry in Russia had mostly started by offering fixed income funds at a time when Russia offered extraordinarily high yields on government debt. Templeton, however, took the unusual move of making its first offering a growth stock fund. Other funds, including fixed income offerings, soon followed.

Franklin Templeton paired the launch of its first funds with a widespread investor education campaign. The strategy recalled Charlie's

At the launch of a Russian fund in 1997, William Pingleton and Mark Mobius posed in front of a statue of Lenin.

MARK MOBIUS

Many people with extraordinary talent came to Franklin with the Templeton acquisition, but Mark Mobius brought a unique reputation. Sporting a shaved head, white suits and a Ph.D. in economics and political science from Massachusetts Institute of Technology, Mobius drew second looks as he traveled the globe searching for investment opportunities in emerging markets.

Mobius joined the Templeton organization in 1987. As president of Templeton Emerging Markets Fund, Inc., he managed the first emerging markets fund listed on the New York Stock Exchange. Starting with nearly $100 million in assets under management, Mobius gained an international reputation for his savvy investments.

Closely associated with Asia, Mobius's investments were hard hit by the Asian financial crisis of 1997 and 1998. But he did not throw in the towel. "Bad times can be good times," he told investors. His optimism paid off. In 1998 Mobius was named the number one global emerging markets fund manager in a Reuters survey.

earliest days in the U.S. market, when he had spent countless hours on the road talking to brokers about the advantages of mutual funds at a time when most investors kept their savings in bank accounts. Forester emphasized that "education is huge in these countries" because of the novelty of mutual funds in a country where many people's savings were still literally kept in mattresses.

It was not long before the company realized the magnitude of the risk it had taken on in Russia. The infrastructure of Russia's financial economy still had a long way to go. Charlie discovered this fact when he visited Moscow and talked to Franklin Templeton's employees. Remembering his own early career in the United States, he suggested the creation of an income fund with Russian bonds. The dividends would be paid to fund shareholders by check. "'Nobody has checks in Russia,'" he was told. People didn't have credit cards either. "There was no way to distribute the dividends," Charlie says.

Russia's lack of development in the financial sector became painfully obvious in 1998 when the economy and stock market suffered a terrible collapse. The stock market lost about 90 percent of its value. Franklin's executive team decided it was time to exit the market. "We were too early," Charlie concluded.

Despite setbacks in Russia, Franklin Templeton's worldwide expansion in the mid-1990s was very successful. By the end of 1997, assets under management in international equities had grown to $107.3 billion. This strong international footprint made the company's investment philosophy increasingly attractive to the growing sector of institutional investors.

Through the mid-1990s, institutional investors, including corporate and public pension funds, were turning to Franklin Templeton. By the end of the fiscal year in 1995, these accounts represented nearly $17 billion in assets, or approximately 13 percent of Franklin Templeton's total assets under management. To keep up with the demand for its products, Franklin Templeton expanded staff at home and abroad. Then suddenly, the company found itself face to face with a new set of challenges.

(L-R): Penny Alexander, Donna Ikeda, Angie Calderon-Loya and Charlie Johnson at Franklin Templeton's holiday party in December 1995. Charlie presented employees of the month with footballs autographed by Joe Montana.

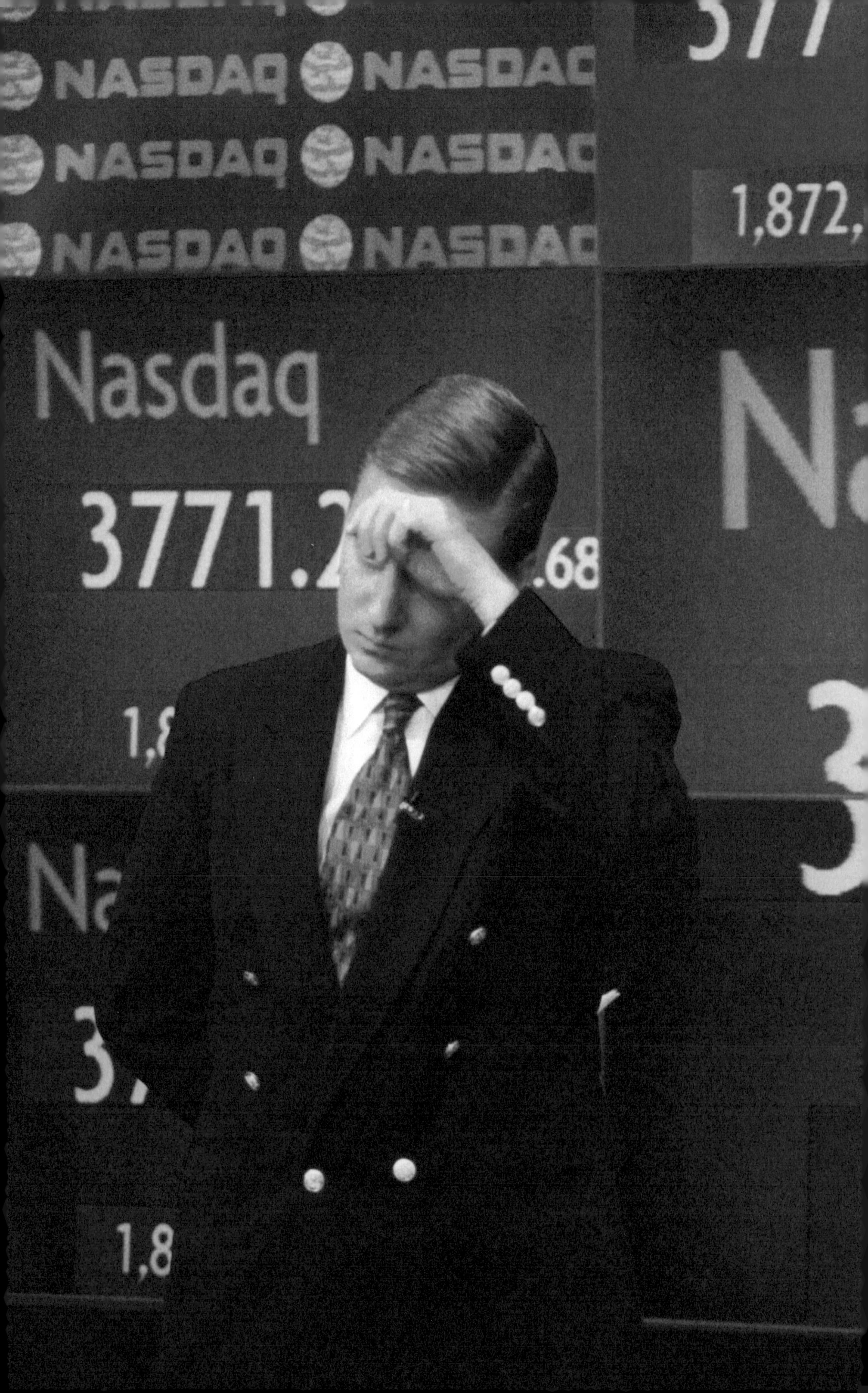
NASDAQ
NASDAQ
NASDAQ
Nasdaq
3771.2
1,872,

Sticking to Principles

How do you know when an Internet investment is just a feeding frenzy?

SEEK ADVICE

The difference between information and knowledge...

The Internet contains a wealth of investment information. So much that it can be confusing. That's where a financial professional can help. An investment representative will take the time to understand your individual needs and long-term investment objectives. Then offer advice tailored to a well-defined strategy and appropriate investments. And many will recommend Franklin Templeton, a leader in the mutual fund industry for over 50 years.

For our free brochure on how to choose an investment professional, "**Getting Advice Can Make All The Difference**," call: 1-800-FRANKLIN.

Franklin Templeton®
777 Mariners Island Blvd.
San Mateo, CA 94404

Prospectuses contain more complete fund information including sales charges and expenses. Please read them carefully before you invest or send money. **Franklin Templeton Distributors, Inc.   www.franklin-templeton.com**

As enthusiasm for Internet stocks increased in the late 1990s, Franklin Templeton cautioned investors to "seek advice." The rush to tech stocks in the late 1990s severely tested Franklin Templeton and ultimately led to a leaner, stronger company.

Opposite: NASDAQ was the barometer of the Internet boom.

Sticking to Principles

Those things that hurt, instruct.

- BENJAMIN FRANKLIN

Since its founding in 1947, Franklin had weathered a number of stock market boom-and-bust cycles by largely sticking to its emphasis on conservative investing for the long term. When pressed, the company responded to popular investment trends only in a careful and measured way. But beginning in the mid-1990s, Franklin's conservative approach fell sharply out of favor.

Starting around 1995, the business press brought word of a new trend, the "Internet" or "dot-com" boom. Any enterprise that based its business upon the Internet, even if it had no record of earnings or even a clear business plan, suddenly became attractive to investors as a front-runner in a new economy that would be based on an online marketplace. Many of these fledgling stocks were bid up to extraordinary valuations.

As the market surged with enthusiasm for the new economy, some Wall Street watchers grew concerned. Speaking to a gathering sponsored by the American Enterprise Institute in December 1996, Federal Reserve Chairman Alan Greenspan expressed concern over the "irrational exuberance" that had fueled a yearlong rise in the Dow Jones Industrial Average from 5,000 to 6,500. This surge drove many people into day trading and online trading, and stock performance once again became a chief topic of watercooler banter. Forrester Research estimated that at the end of 1997 nearly three million investors were involved in online trading.

The fund companies that jumped onto this growth stock boom did very well for a time. The most striking example was Kinetics Internet Fund, managed by Ryan Jacob, which grew from $200,000 in assets in December 1997 to a dizzying $450 million by early 1999, posting returns of over 200 percent during 1998–99. More established companies also launched aggressive, technology-based funds, sometimes reluctantly. One prominent technology investor told *Fortune* magazine, "I buy these stocks because I live in a competitive universe, and I can't beat my benchmarks without them." According to this same broker, "You either participate in this mania, or you go out of business."

Buying stock in many of these new Internet companies required the type of trend-chasing, high-risk approach to investing that Charlie and Rupert, Jr., had never believed in. Analysts enthralled with new economy rhetoric told Franklin's management, "You guys don't get it anymore." As Chuck remembers, "Anything of value fell out of favor, and it was horrific." The Internet wave had the effect of putting Franklin Templeton on the defensive. "We had always been known as a bond house," says Deborah Gatzek, the firm's general counsel in these years. "So people were turning away from us at the time because we didn't have really sexy technology or growth products." After working hard through the 1980s to build a prominent profile, Franklin found itself losing touch with the market. Discouraged by the situation, Harmon Burns remarked one day, "I don't understand. People talk about the industry, and we never get mentioned. It is like we fell off the earth." According to Jenny Bolt, "That was what it was like. Suddenly we weren't on the radar screen."

Franklin did not miss the growth stock boom entirely. It had one small-capitalization growth fund, started in the early 1990s by

Ed Jamieson, that did very well during this period. As Jamieson describes it, "We decided to make it a growth fund because Franklin Templeton had so many value funds. That was a stroke of luck, because the whole growth market took off for the next eight years. It was a huge run." Managed with the help of Michael McCarthy, the fund stood out as the exception that proved the rule that Franklin's culture was not generally conducive to joining a feeding frenzy for risky stocks. Ed Jamieson recalls, "We got tons of money into Small Cap Growth Fund because we had this huge distribution force and one fund that was really doing well. . . . It was a very, very exciting period for Mike and me, and we had top-quartile performance for probably seven of those eight years. . . . It was kind of an anomaly, because the firm was struggling, and we had a hot product." For some in the company, the success of Franklin Small Cap Growth Fund was a reminder of how important diversification is not only to the individual investor, but to the investment management firm as well.

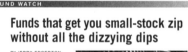

FUND WATCH

Funds that get you small-stock zip without all the dizzying dips

BY JERRY EDGERTON

THE LONG-AWAITED SMALL-STOCK revival suddenly seems to be under way. From the start of 1994 through March of this year, the big-company S&P 500 index smoked the small-company Russell 2000 by 75.9% to 39.4%. But from April 1 to Oct. 17, the Russell rebounded and outran the S&P 500 32.3% to 25.4%. And even after the steep drop that hit the market in late October, many Wall Street seers expect the little guys to lead the pack for the next six to 12 months on the strength of faster earnings growth. Overall, analysts see average profit increases of 20% for small stocks next year vs. 10% or so for large companies. One reason:

ALL FUND DATA AS OF OCT. 17

The strength of the U.S. dollar and weakness of many Southeast Asian economies are crimping profits for large multinational companies. But those factors generally don't affect smaller firms, which tend to get most of their sales in the U.S. "Our Prudential forecast is for 10% earnings growth on the S&P 500 in 1998—a level that will disappoint many investors," says Melissa Brown, head of quantitative analysis for Prudential Securities. "I think there is a good chance that small-company stocks will escape that kind of earnings disappointment."

To help fund investors benefit from the resurgence of small growth stocks, we identified four portfolios that have produced high returns without the wild swings that roil the most aggressive small-company funds. Those risky "momentum" funds seek the fastest-growing companies they can find and are willing to pay almost any price to get them. The funds profiled here, by contrast, favor growth stocks selling at what the managers consider reasonable levels; one, Managers Special Equity, includes a dose of super-fast-growing, high-priced stocks along with tamer picks.

To find these standouts, we screened Morningstar's universe of 343 funds that specialize in fast-growing small companies and an additional 141 small-company funds that blend growth and value styles. The four funds you see here outperformed the small-company average over the past one, three and five years. Just as important, they don't rely on the highest-priced stocks that fall the most in a downturn.

Each did better than the average small-company growth fund during the two most recent small-stock meltdowns (see the table on page 54 for these and other key performance figures). Here are profiles of our four picks in order of their five-year records.

Franklin Small Cap Growth I
At first glance, this $2.3 billion fund seems uncomfortably large for a small-capper, having pulled in $1 billion in fresh cash from investors over the past year. But lead manager Edward Jamieson, 49, has coped with the flood of new money by increasing the number of issues in the fund to about 150 from 100. He has no trouble tracking the added stocks, he says, because he has the help of the 25 analysts who work for this and other Franklin funds.

Moreover, Jamieson insists that the fund's expansion hasn't forced him to shift his focus or lower his standards. He still targets small companies and attempts to buy them at a price/earnings ratio lower than their annual earnings growth rate. The median market value of the stocks in the portfolio is $894 million—just about

Ed Jamieson launched Franklin Small Cap Growth Fund before the Internet boom began. Through the 1990s, the fund enjoyed great success while many other Franklin Templeton funds fell out of favor as dot-com fever took hold of the equity markets.

While Franklin Templeton also started a few specialty funds, the company largely managed the crisis of being "out of style" by simply sticking to its core investment strategy, which had worked well for so many years. Gatzek recalls people wondering, "'What can we do to catch up?' There really wasn't a lot. You could try to buy somebody, but of course any growth house at that time would have had a huge multiple." The pundits on Wall Street and in Silicon Valley predicted that the Internet would eliminate the need for brokers. During a leadership conference, Greg remembers, "People were saying we better get with it. We better go out and start a Schwab or buy a Schwab."

Charlie responded, "I have been around for a long time, and I remember the Nifty 50 in the 1960s, which were the large growth stocks—computers, pharmaceutical companies and so on. Everybody jumped in after them, and then they crashed." Charlie understood the psychology and the rhythms of the market. His message to employees: Stick to the game plan.

For Franklin Templeton the morale crisis was worsened by the company's location at the edge of Silicon Valley. Employees went home and had dinner with their friends who were working for dot-com companies. "We kept reinforcing the message that advice is not dead," says Greg. At one point, Franklin ran an ad that depicted a mousetrap baited with cheese and computer mice headed for the cheese. The ad copy asked: "How do you know when an Internet investment is just a feeding frenzy?" The answer: "Seek advice."

THE ASIAN FINANCIAL CRISIS

The late 1990s' tech stock boom that caused Franklin Templeton to lose favor with investors was compounded by an Asian economic crisis that delivered a hard hit to the international funds managed by Templeton. The remarkable growth of various East and Southeast Asian countries during the 1980s and 1990s was one of the most notable economic success stories of the 20th century. South Korea, for example, achieved annual growth rates in real GDP of over 9 percent from 1980 to 1990. Malaysia's real GDP grew an average of 7 percent per year between 1980 and 1995. While many acknowledged that such extraordinary rates of expansion were bound to slow down eventually, few predicted the complete crash that occurred during mid-to-late 1997.

The reasons for the crisis were various and complex, although the immediate cause was the extreme dependence on short-term credit among the hardest-hit countries of Indonesia, South Korea, Malaysia, the Philippines and Thailand. When negative economic news from the region began to appear in early 1997 (a missed loan payment by a South Korean steel conglomerate, for instance, and a cooldown in the overheated real estate market in Thailand), a chain-reaction panic started among international lenders. As credit evaporated, the affected countries saw the value of their currencies collapse, partly as a result of their own governments' rush to purchase foreign exchange to pay off the short-term loans being called for repayment. The boom times in Asia slammed to a halt. Growth rates declined, and emerging market stock indexes plummeted.

In the offices of Templeton Worldwide, the impact of the crisis was swift and harsh. Coming upon the heels of a similar Latin American currency crisis in 1994–95, the resulting fund losses put under a critical spotlight the most prominent fund managers in the Templeton group, Mark Mobius and Mark Holowesko. Mobius's various emerging markets funds were particularly hard hit. By May of 1998, a Korea-focused fund started in 1996 was down 67 percent. An Indian fund and a Japanese fund launched the year before each declined 27 percent. A Thai fund also started in 1997 right before the Asia crisis plunged 53 percent. By October 1998 Franklin's flagship emerging markets fund, Templeton Developing Markets Trust I, was down over 36 percent. Holowesko's more conservative Templeton Growth Fund I was down as well. Despite these numbers, Charlie remained confident in the company's strategy. He reiterated that Franklin Templeton was in Asia for the long haul.

While Holowesko was not as publicly well known at this time, Mobius was quite comfortable in the media glare. With his vague resemblance to Yul Brynner, loquacious personality, a Ph.D. in economics and political science, and legendary travel schedule, Mobius had become a media darling during the boom years of emerging market investing in the early 1990s. Franklin Templeton had contributed to his high profile by featuring him in a number of international advertisements. Mobius seemed the personification of the swashbuckling international investor, right down to the Gulfstream IV jet the company purchased so he could more easily shuttle his research team around the world for visits to investment prospects. Long based in Singapore and a member of Sir John Templeton's team at Templeton, Galbraith and Hansberger since 1987, Mobius practiced a classic form of value investing that was squarely within the Templeton mold. As he described it, "The question we ask is: 'Where are the bargains?' If there are no bargains, then we are not interested. We are often asked: 'How much cash do you have in your funds?' But that is the wrong question. The best is: 'How many bargains do you have in your funds?'"

This relentless search for bargain stocks, along with an eagerness to seek them in previously obscure markets like Russia, Turkey and Vietnam, made Mobius a pioneer in emerging market investing who often delivered extraordinary returns. In 1997 the 10-year annualized return of Templeton Emerging Markets Fund was almost 25 percent. Investors responded by suddenly pouring immense amounts of money into emerging markets funds during the mid-1990s. In 1990 there were only seven such funds with inflows of $136 million. Thanks in large part to Mobius's efforts, by 1996 there were over 200 emerging markets funds. As one professional investor once remarked to *SmartMoney* magazine, "If [Mobius] didn't exist, the emerging markets world would have to invent him."

As other value investors found to their chagrin, however, the value-based approach to picking stocks simply did not work very well during the late 1990s. Mobius's main problem was that when the Asian markets crashed at the end of 1997, he quickly made large bets on various distressed Asian stocks. Unfortunately, rather than enjoying the rebound he expected, the Asian markets continued to fall. In his letter to Templeton Developing Markets Trust shareholders at the end of 1998, his usual confidence seemed a bit shaken as he admitted, "There is no way to mince words about the fund's performance." Nonetheless, he determinedly urged investors to always take the long view: "You have to remember that the declines in Asia did not suddenly destroy the incredible work ethic typically evident in these countries or instantly rob them of the great strides they have made in education and infrastructure development." True to form, when speaking to a reporter that year about the advice he gave to a sister-in-law who was unhappy with her investment in his fund, Mobius insisted, "I told her to buy more. When these markets come back, they're really going to pop."

HARD DECISIONS

While Mobius and others waited for the market in Asia to recover, the executives at Franklin Templeton realized they needed to make some changes. When they gathered for meetings in Lyford Cay in the Bahamas in February 1998, Marty Flanagan told Charlie Johnson, "We need to spend a few minutes." When the two had a chance to sit down, Flanagan told Charlie, "We have a problem. It looks as if expenses are surging out of control."

Charlie listened carefully. Since Franklin acquired Templeton in 1992, he had grown to respect Flanagan's judgment and to understand why John Templeton had given the young man so much responsibility. Charlie asked Flanagan to pull together the data in a memo for the senior executives: Charlie, Rupert and Harmon Burns. Soon the analysis by Flanagan and his staff was clear to everyone on the executive team. Rapid growth in the mid-1990s had exceeded the capacity of the company's infrastructure to keep pace. To avoid service problems, the company had put people and resources into place to get the job done one way or another, and not always with the greatest efficiency. The expansion of the organization by acquisition and growth had confused lines of authority and financial accountability, contributing to the increase in costs. As Charlie put it, through the boom years "our challenge was to hire people and train them and get them on the job. Then all of a sudden that wasn't our challenge anymore, but it took everyone awhile to switch gears."

Flanagan suggested the need for a new structure that would clarify the company's vision and objectives and prioritize the allocation of capital and resources. Specifically, the company needed to set clear financial objectives to enhance shareholder value. It also needed to develop an efficient global operations infrastructure and accelerate the transition to a global system that would enable digital distribution of information to everyone in the organization.

Flanagan's memo offered a number of suggestions for further study. He pointed out that the company's incentive programs had become misaligned. Too many people were being compensated for expanding staff rather than for performance. In addition, it was increasingly important to view all operations as part of a global system and to locate services in the lowest-cost environment. Specifically, the pace of expansion in the high-cost San Francisco Bay Area had to be slowed. Other parts of the United States offered a less expensive environment for labor and office space.

The final step in the effort to rebalance Franklin's financial position, according to Flanagan's memo, was to raise cash and then establish a more disciplined process for allocating capital. Franklin was particularly short of cash in the United States in early 1998, so the memo proposed the securitization of the loans held by Franklin's automobile financing unit.

Through the spring and summer of 1998, the senior management team moved forward on many of the long-range issues discussed in Flanagan's memo, but there was no sense of crisis. The company's revenues were strong for the first two quarters of fiscal year 1998, although they dropped in the spring as some of the company's fund shareholders cashed out to put their money into the surging U.S. stock market. Then in July, redemptions outpaced sales. The $10.8 billion Mutual Shares Fund, for example, had net redemptions of $114 million in July. Management's perspective changed dramatically in September when corporate finance delivered the news that total assets under management had declined to $208.6 billion from $226 billion the previous year, and earnings were projected to fall by 50 percent. "That is unacceptable," Charlie told the management team. Immediately, the company accelerated its cost-cutting efforts. A planned expansion to add customer service operations in San Diego was canceled.

≈At the same time, the company launched a review designed to trim $150 million from the company's operating budget. To focus on streamlining business processes, Franklin Templeton's leadership asked the management consulting firm of McKinsey & Company in the fall of 1998 to undertake a "clean sheet" analysis with senior staff to help redesign the company's operations. The clean sheet process prompted managers to challenge all of their assumptions about how they were doing business.

≈At a meeting in Toronto in March 1999, Jenny Bolt, with Wendy Harrington from McKinsey, led a team effort to identify opportunities for quick improvements as well as long-term initiatives. The group focused on how work flowed between Franklin's various customer groups—financial institutions, financial advisors, wirehouses, direct shareholders—and the company. The group discussed opportunities to automate more processes using improved software.

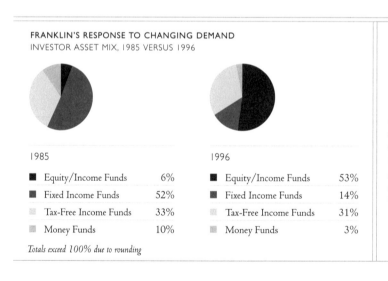

FRANKLIN'S RESPONSE TO CHANGING DEMAND
INVESTOR ASSET MIX, 1985 VERSUS 1996

1985			1996		
■ Equity/Income Funds	6%		■ Equity/Income Funds	53%	
■ Fixed Income Funds	52%		■ Fixed Income Funds	14%	
Tax-Free Income Funds	33%		Tax-Free Income Funds	31%	
Money Funds	10%		Money Funds	3%	

Totals exceed 100% due to rounding

Between 1985 and 1996, the mix of Franklin's assets under management shifted from predominantly fixed income to a better diversified mix of equity and income funds.

After the Toronto meeting, a companywide initiative was launched. "It was the beginning of a major shift for the institution," says Flanagan. "We were no longer a family." It was not unlike the shift that Franklin went through when Charlie and Rupert bought Winfield in 1973, an organization-defining moment. Greg points out that the company became more performance oriented. "We adopted specific performance metrics and began to match rewards to outcomes." The process sparked new ways of working with greater accountability and a commitment to continuous improvement, performance reviews and succession planning. Sometimes it was hard on people. "It makes you a little less friendly," says Greg, "but I think employees would rather have the honesty and direct feedback." This approach also leveled the playing field, and many employees felt it created a fairer system for compensation.

In January 1999, Charlie sent an email to all employees announcing that the company would eliminate approximately 560 positions by consolidating regional processing centers and refocusing business units. This was a hard decision for Charlie and Rupert. For years, the Johnsons had promoted from within, rewarding performance and loyalty. They were proud of the longevity of many of the company's employees. Marty Flanagan says, "Charlie knew when we got there what had to be done. It was not something he liked to do on the people side of the business, but he knew

FRANKLIN TEMPLETON'S TEAM
NUMBER OF EMPLOYEES, 1992–1999

With acquisitions and internal growth, the Franklin Templeton team grew steadily in the 1990s. After integrating the company's domestic technology for shareholder services and support in 1998, Franklin Templeton trimmed its workforce.

it was a necessity for the institution, an obligation to the other individuals, the shareholders and the clients. It was gut-wrenching, but it turned into all hands on deck."

Management focused on eliminating positions through attrition and a hiring freeze, closing out any open positions. As Charlie had pointed out to employees, the staff reduction was possible "because we are beginning to realize the benefits of our conversion onto a single shareholder system." Franklin Templeton accelerated the move of service operations out of San Mateo to Rancho Cordova. The company offered employees the opportunity to move, but many had deep roots in the Bay Area or spouses who had jobs. The company also provided outplacement services if employees chose to leave the company. In the midst of the dot-com explosion, the demand for skilled employees in the Bay Area was high. Franklin Templeton gave generous severance packages, mitigating the financial impact of layoffs on many employees. But when the last days arrived, it was tough. Charlie met individually with many of the longtime employees in his office. When Judy Faasisila came to say good-bye, she and Charlie talked about the early days in the transfer agency. It was an emotional moment for both of them.

Charlie's January email to all employees also emphasized the frugality that had been a hallmark of the company's history. "We all need to focus our efforts on continually improving customer service, streamlining our business processes, controlling expenses and ensuring our resources are allocated to those activities that best service our clients."

While Franklin Templeton searched for ways to be more efficient, the company also undertook a major review of its product line. Between the beginning of 1998 and the middle of 1999, the company eliminated 23 U.S. mutual funds and 10 non-U.S. funds. Franklin Templeton also developed two new growth funds to meet the demand for this kind of investment opportunity.

The positive results of instituting these changes soon became apparent. In May, Charlie reported to the company's executives that changes to business practices had saved Franklin Templeton $50 million since the year began. "Many employees that I spoke to thought the cost-cutting initiatives signaled the end of the company," Charlie said. "The truth of the matter is that Franklin Templeton went through a stage that many companies experience after a period of rapid growth sparked by a large acquisition." Indeed, by the end of the fiscal year in 1999, the company had reduced the run rate on expenses by over $150 million a year and seemed poised for a new era in its history.

⌒Throughout this period, management worked to keep morale up, especially among the portfolio managers. "This came from my father and my uncle," says Chuck. "They bucked up everybody else and said, 'Hang in there. Don't change. You will always come out of one of these cycles okay....' The temptation is always, when things are at their darkest, to start lightening up on your holdings. Then you are dead, because you never come back. If you stick to your guns, sooner or later the cycle will turn. They [Charlie and Rupert] afforded most of the groups the latitude to do that."

⌒As Charlie had demonstrated throughout his career, his belief in doing what was best for investors in the long term could not be compromised by market trends. Speaking to the staff in St. Petersburg, Greg repeated his father's message. Echoing the sentiments of the main character in the movie *Apollo 13*, he said, "This may well be our finest hour." As all of Franklin Templeton's executives tried to make clear, the early years of the Internet explosion were a painful reminder that doing what was right was sometimes immensely unpopular.

A NEW LOOK TO FRANKLIN TEMPLETON'S LEADERSHIP

The major restructuring that began with Marty Flanagan's warning in 1998 also led to executive team changes that were unveiled just before Thanksgiving 1999. Recognizing that new investments in technology could produce substantial cost savings in operations, Franklin Templeton went outside its own ranks to recruit a chief information officer. Allen Gula, the chief technology officer and executive vice president at KeyCorp, a Cleveland-based bank holding company, came with a mandate to refocus the company on the strategic value of technology. As Y2K and the Internet forced the retirement of some legacy systems, Gula worked with IBM to accelerate the company's transition to more robust systems. He also introduced processes for assessing the value of new technologies to the business. Gula reported directly to Charlie, underscoring the importance of technology to Franklin Templeton's future.

The company then announced it would reorganize top management to create a three-person Office of the Chairman and a four-person Office of the President. The Office of the Chairman included Charlie, Rupert and Harmon Burns. Chuck, Greg and Marty Flanagan would be a team in the Office of the President, along with Gula. Chuck would become president of the international division. Greg would serve as president of the U.S. retail and institutional businesses. Flanagan would be the company's chief financial officer and also supervise investment management and the Canadian businesses.

The creation of the Office of the President set up a three-way horse race for the future (Gula was in a key strategic role, but not a candidate to head the company). Flanagan's leadership at Templeton and financial acumen made him a well-qualified leader with the potential to go further. Greg's experience in marketing, sales and investment management gave him a strong perspective on the company's competitive position. Chuck's leadership in the development of Franklin's early technology, and in the company's international ventures, marketing and acquisitions, positioned him as a strong candidate.

None of the men in the race were under any illusions. Though they were all being tested, Charlie made it clear by his manner and his own style of management that he expected teamwork and cooperation. Some employees were skeptical, however. They feared that management by committee would delay decision making, confuse lines of authority and divide loyalties within the various parts of the business. Charlie, Rupert and Harmon had faith in the individuals on the team. If there were problems, they would be there to mentor this new executive team.

As the new executive team began to develop its style of collaboration, Franklin Templeton's growth rebounded. The rapid expansion of retirement accounts in the United States, fueled by investments in 401(k) programs, combined with improving markets abroad to drive asset growth.

For Franklin Templeton, growth in 401(k) activity grew out of the company's institutional business. In the early 1980s, many U.S. companies had begun to develop 401(k) retirement programs for their employees. As these programs proliferated, mutual fund companies began to offer to administer these plans as a way to market their investment products. The entry of several big mutual fund companies, including Fidelity and Vanguard, into this market posed a major threat to both Franklin Templeton and the employee benefits consultants who had historically filled this niche.

Franklin Templeton followed an interesting strategy to break into the 401(k) market. It began to form strategic alliances with employee benefits consultants to allow them to compete with Fidelity and Vanguard by providing an array of investment products from different companies. As Rick Frisbie, then senior vice president for Institutional Sales, described it, "We helped the consultants, and they helped us get into the 401(k) market we'd been boxed out of." The strategy worked. Soon, the employee benefits consultants were putting pressure on the mutual fund companies to offer more than just their own proprietary products in the 401(k) plans for which they also provided recordkeeping services. By 1999 Franklin Templeton was available in 23 percent of 401(k) plans across the United States. The popularity of Franklin Templeton in 401(k) plans led to increased demand from annuity providers, as well as for IRA accounts.

A SECOND LOOK AT B SHARES

By early 1998, Franklin's difficulties in selling funds through banks were being resolved. More focused marketing efforts were paying off, and with the combined acquisitions of Templeton and Mutual Series, investors began to recognize Franklin Templeton as a strong equity fund provider. While still lagging Putnam by a large margin, fund sales in bank channels rose to their previous 1993 peak of $4 billion. Intent on continuing this momentum, the fund boards voted to offer a B share option and to rename Class I and Class II shares to Class A and Class C, respectively.

    Following the merger with Mutual Series, Franklin faced a dilemma similar to what it faced in 1994 after the acquisition of Templeton. This time, Franklin opted for a more rationalized and standardized system of sales charges that applied across all its fund offerings. In August 1998, Franklin raised the front-end sales charge for Franklin and Mutual Series Class A equity fund shares to 5.75 percent. This move brought the sales charge for these funds in line with the Templeton group of funds. It also brought the sales charges for Franklin funds in line with its major competitors. This change was designed mainly to enhance Franklin's ability to support its broker network. Finally, the required minimum investment amount was also raised to a still comparatively low $1,000. Class II (now C) shares remained little changed, with a 1 percent front-end sales charge and higher annual expenses than Class I (now A) shares, along with a contingent deferred sales charge. These changes to the share classes helped position Franklin Templeton more strongly in the market, but suddenly the market itself turned in the company's favor.

THE BUBBLE BURSTS

The tech market in the United States reached its peak in 1999. That year the NASDAQ Index shot up 84 percent while the S&P 500 Index rose "only" 15 percent. At the top of the boom in January 2000, the market capitalization of U.S. stocks was measured at $17 trillion, 1.7 times the value of American gross domestic product. Reflecting the broadening of ownership in the economy, half of all U.S. households owned stock in 1999. Investing had become the national pastime.

    Over 60 funds boasted returns above 100 percent in 1999. The assets of these funds were either entirely or mostly invested in technology stocks. By contrast, just six funds had posted such high numbers at the end of 1998. With the arrival of the new millennium, it seemed the flow of instant riches from the market would never cease. By early March 2000, the NASDAQ was up another 25 percent.

But then there was a momentum shift. The expressions of concern about an overheated market that had surfaced intermittently since 1995 finally began to be heard. It was Abby Joseph Cohen, the chief market strategist at Goldman Sachs, who is often credited with triggering the initial collapse of the tech boom. She had become a media favorite for her aggressively bullish stance on tech stocks throughout the 1990s. One analyst described her as "the best-known market guru, and she's been right for a long time." In the final days of March, however, she had a grim message for all the tech bulls: "For the first time in a decade, our model portfolio is no longer recommending an overweighted position in technology. Many of the technology shares were given the respect they deserve over the last 18 months, and are no longer undervalued."

In April the market started to falter. On Monday, April 10, 2000, a sell-off of technology stocks began. On Friday, April 14, the Dow plunged 616 points to close the day at 10,307. Altogether, the weeklong slide erased nearly a quarter of the NASDAQ's market capitalization. Nearly $1 trillion in wealth had evaporated. Within a year, the NASDAQ was down nearly 70 percent from its previous highs, and the Dow Jones had lost over 20 percent. Because of the increased popularization of stock ownership that had occurred over the last 15 years, the end of the dot-com mania exacted a greater toll on more individual investors than previous such downturns.

The bursting of the dot-com bubble ultimately vindicated Franklin Templeton's investing philosophy, but not before more pain. Of the top 10 fund companies in the United States, only two suffered outflows during the first half of 2000. Franklin was one of them, with net redemptions totaling nearly $4.5 billion. Yet value-oriented funds were starting to make a comeback. During the first eight months of 2000, for instance, as the NASDAQ was collapsing and the S&P earned around 1.5 percent,

Mutual Shares Fund rose over 3.5 percent. Greg Johnson expressed confidence that the worst was over. "You need a better one-year [performance] number before you start to see any real shift in flows," he told a reporter. "We are getting very close to that stage." By August 2000, with its stock price now severely beaten down, analysts were finally beginning to recommend Franklin Resources as a good buy.

⌇The crash of the stock market also led to a new round of consolidation in the mutual fund industry. In September, Chase Manhattan Bank announced that it would buy J. P. Morgan & Co. Franklin looked for opportunities to make its own strategic move.

BUYING FIDUCIARY TRUST INTERNATIONAL

Down markets always provide opportunities to investors looking for value. That was as true in 2000 as it was in 1931, when Fiduciary Trust was founded to provide investors with a trustworthy investment manager. Over the next 43 years, the company grew, and in May of 1974 it moved into a new worldwide headquarters in four upper floors in the newly completed World Trade Center. Fiduciary furthered its expansion in 1977 when the company merged with Davis, Palmer & Biggs, a New York investment counseling firm. Over the next two decades, the firm continued to grow by focusing on high net-worth individuals and families and providing investment management services to the foundations, nonprofits and other charitable organizations that benefited from the philanthropy of Fiduciary's clients.

⌇Anne Tatlock was at the helm of Fiduciary in 2000 when the company began to talk to Franklin about a possible acquisition. Tatlock had been among a small minority of women working on Wall Street when she began her career at Smith Barney in the 1960s. She moved to Fiduciary in 1984 to work in the international arena. In January 1990, she took over the management of the company's international equities team, and her executive responsibilities continued to grow. She was named CEO in September 1999.

⌇Tatlock's first realization that Fiduciary might need to find a strategic partner came shortly before she became CEO, when technology was added to her list of assignments. Starting with little background, she immersed herself in the issues and before long realized "it was a money pit." The company needed advanced systems for global accounting and reporting to clients. At the time, the financial press carried stories about the hundreds of millions of dollars that firms like J. P. Morgan were spending on systems. To Tatlock it was clear that Fiduciary didn't have the scale in systems or people to compete effectively in the coming marketplace. She and Bill Yun, the company's president, discussed the options. Downsizing and becoming less global seemed to offer a profitable, but unacceptable alternative. "We were in strong agreement that being global was a 'must,'" she says.

Fiduciary's board hired Goldman Sachs to do a study of the strengths and weaknesses of the business. The report highlighted Fiduciary's vulnerabilities: its lack of distribution capability, no presence in the mutual fund business and an inadequate technology platform. The board asked Tatlock to recommend a strategy. With ambivalence, she gradually began talking to Milton Berlinski at Goldman Sachs about possible acquirers. The list was soon whittled down to three, including Franklin Templeton.

FIDUCIARY TRUST
INTERNATIONAL

In 1931 Grenville Clark and Elihu Root, Jr., prominent New York lawyers and citizens, founded Fiduciary Trust. Reacting to the excesses of the New York banking industry in the 1920s, the two men resolved not to make commercial loans or underwrite securities. Instead, they committed themselves to investment management, pure and simple. To inspire confidence, they recruited Pierre Jay, who had been the bank commissioner for Massachusetts as well as the first chairman of the Federal Reserve Bank of New York, to become chairman of Fiduciary Trust.

The company grew by handling the portfolios of some of the richest Americans and by keeping an eye on the global scene. Within four years of its founding, it had clients in 12 countries and 30 states, and more than $60 million in assets under management.

Fiduciary also played a leading role in international investment, becoming an advisor to the United Nations shortly after its inception in 1947 and establishing a London office to better serve the UN in 1961.

ANNE TATLOCK

Wall Street welcomed few women in the early 1960s when Anne Tatlock began her career. Nevertheless, Tatlock went to New York University at night to complete a master's degree in economics. Her employer, Smith Barney, wouldn't take women into its Management Training Program at the time, but Tatlock won a job in the Investment Advisory Department.

A focused researcher with strong analytical and communication skills, Tatlock soon won the attention of her bosses and was allowed to shadow the Management Training Program on an "unofficial" basis. In 1974 she began managing institutional accounts and ultimately the department. She soon became one of the highest-ranking women in the company and on Wall Street.

The November 1976 charter issue of *Working Woman* magazine featured rising stars on Wall Street, including Anne Tatlock (bottom center).

The first meeting between the two companies took place at the Harvard Club in New York in July 2000. After the meeting, Yun and Tatlock were surprised by their impressions of Charlie Johnson. "I could have been working with this man my whole life," Tatlock mused. "He is so like everybody at Fiduciary." Still, she was sure she was not interested in a deal. As she and Yun completed their meetings with the two other firms on Berlinski's list, however, they both concluded what was now becoming obvious: "Everything we put on our list that we want is at Franklin." A management meeting was organized in

San Mateo in September with all the senior people. "I decided that day that it was right," Tatlock remembers. Within six weeks, the two companies had reached a firm agreement.

The deal that was announced in October 2000 stipulated that Franklin Templeton would acquire Fiduciary Trust International for $825 million in stock. Franklin Templeton hoped that Fiduciary would give it the platform for servicing and managing the assets of high net-worth individuals as well as the institutions that they were associated with. The deal also gave Franklin Templeton greater clout in the competition for business with defined benefit and defined pension markets in Europe, Asia and Latin America. Altogether, the Fiduciary acquisition seemed to add one more enterprise with similar values and a complementary structure to the expanding global enterprise of Franklin Templeton.

According to the word on the Street in the fall of 2000, Franklin Templeton was talking to other organizations as well. In October, the company was reported to be holding merger talks with the giant German insurance company Allianz AG. Charlie insisted to the press that with the completion of the Fiduciary deal he hoped to "demonstrate to the world that when we said we were not for sale, we were not for sale." Franklin Templeton underscored this point in October by acquiring Bissett & Associates Investment Management, Ltd. Bissett complemented Franklin Templeton's existing operations in Canada and, like Fiduciary, gave the company access to high net-worth investors as well as pension plans, foundations and financial institutions. Shortly after completing the Fiduciary transaction in April 2001, Franklin Templeton launched a stock buyback program, announcing that the company intended to repurchase nearly 3 million shares at a cost of $129 million. For those investors who continued to own Franklin stock, it was a promising moment.

LOOKING AHEAD

With the acquisition of Fiduciary and Bissett, Franklin reasserted its independence and signaled that it was prepared for future growth. In the

Bay Area, the company was also setting the stage for a new era. Franklin Templeton had long ago outgrown the facilities at 777 Mariners Island Boulevard and now had offices scattered throughout San Mateo. To hold meetings, employees had to drive and search for parking. Increasingly, busy people wouldn't do it. "You would just do everything by conference call," Penny Alexander remembers. But that wasn't good for teamwork. When a nearby shopping center closed, Franklin Templeton bid for the space, but didn't win the auction. "That was very scary when that happened," says Alexander, "because there wasn't a whole lot of land on the Peninsula and people worried that we would have to move to the East Bay." Franklin Templeton got a break, however, when the company that owned the Bay Meadows Race Track in San Mateo decided to sell a major portion of its real estate. Franklin Templeton was able to purchase the property and immediately pulled a team together to begin planning the new campus.

Employees moved into the global headquarters in the summer of 2001. "Once we got here, a phenomenal sense of community came almost overnight," says Alexander. "You ran into people in the cafeteria that you hadn't seen in years." These kinds of casual interactions accelerated the exchange of information and sparked new ideas. By the fall of 2001, optimism and excitement were running high throughout the business.

San Mateo Mayor
John Lee joined
CEO Charlie Johnson
in a ribbon-cutting
ceremony to celebrate
the 2001 opening of
Franklin Templeton's
new global headquar-
ters at One Franklin
Parkway in San Mateo.

September 11, 2001

LIFE DURING WARTIME REBUILDING

Back to work: Fiduciary's Anne Tatlock and Bill Yun at their new headquarters in Midtown Manhattan.

SHATTERED, NOT BROKEN

Like many financial service companies operating in the
World Trade Center, Fiduciary Trust was hit hard.
But it had one thing many rivals didn't: a backup plan.

70 FORBES • October 15, 2001

On September 11, 2001,
the world changed when
terrorists piloted airliners
into the north and south
towers of the World
Trade Center. In the
aftermath of the attack,
employees across the
company pulled together
to support their
colleagues in New York.

Opposite: View of lower
Manhattan from the
Hudson River, pre-2001.

September 11, 2001

We have emerged from September 11 with a renewed sense of purpose, yet we live constantly with the memories of the colleagues and friends we lost that day.

- ANNE TATLOCK, CEO
FIDUCIARY TRUST INTERNATIONAL

Early Tuesday morning, September 11, 2001, Anne Tatlock boarded a bus in Omaha, Nebraska, along with Warren Buffett and a group of CEOs. They were scheduled to tour Offutt Air Force Base and visit the Strategic Air Command Center. Upon arrival, military officers stepped onto the bus and informed the group that an incident had just occurred at the World Trade Center in New York, and suggested that anyone involved with any activity there might want to break off from the tour. With 650 employees working in the upper floors of the south tower, Tatlock hurried to the base quarters to find out what was going on.

In New York, at 8:46 a.m., many of Fiduciary's employees felt the blast of heat from the explosion of American Airlines Flight 11 as it slammed into the north tower 131 feet away. Many had lived through the World Trade Center garage bombing in February 1993. Since then, they had prepared for an evacuation. At the direction of former CEO Larry Huntington, every employee had a flashlight and fresh batteries in case of a loss of power. The safety training provided by the Port Authority emphasized the importance of waiting in your office if you were not in immediate danger, to avoid the crush of thousands of people trying to leave the building at once.

 On September 11, however, Fiduciary's managers quickly decided to get everyone out. Alayne Gentul, director of Human Resources, began herding people from all of Fiduciary's floors toward the stairwells. From the 90th floor, they descended to the sky lobby at the 78th floor and then waited for the express elevators to the main lobby. Others, dismayed by the crowd in the sky lobby, continued down the stairs.

 Unfortunately, not everyone left. Instead of stepping onto the last car going down, Ed Emery, Fiduciary's training director, went back upstairs. He and Gentul wanted to ensure that employees were evacuating. Other people upstairs were also trying to help get everyone out. Bob Mattson, a senior vice president, had been one of the last to leave in 1993, rescued from the roof by helicopter. On September 11, he once again stayed to help.

 While people upstairs were trying to help employees leave, building security officials in the ground floor lobby and on the 78th floor were telling everyone that despite the fire in the north tower, the south tower was safe and secure. People should return to their offices, they said. Encouraged by these announcements, Donovan Cowan and Doris Torres stepped into an elevator. Donovan had his finger pressed on the button for the 97th floor when suddenly an explosion knocked him off his feet.

 Just at that moment in Omaha, Anne Tatlock was watching the news on television in an officers' lounge. On the screen, she saw smoke billowing from the north tower. Then she watched in horror as United Airlines Flight 175, the second plane, traveling at 545 miles per hour, tipped its wings and sliced into the south tower just below Fiduciary's offices. A ball of fire burst through the building on the other side. "All of their faces suddenly came to me," she remembers. Immediately, she began calling her staff, hoping someone would answer.

The plane had cut through the 77th, 78th and 79th floors. Dozens of people waiting in the sky lobby for elevators were killed instantly. Cowan and Torres, protected inside an elevator, were thrown from side to side and engulfed in a wave of tremendous heat, but they survived. People on the upper floors of the building were thrown against walls or furniture by the impact. Almost immediately they felt the heat and smelled the smoke from the inferno below. Believing that all stairwells going down were blocked, they called friends, relatives and 911 for help. They stuffed clothes under the doors and in the air vents to block the smoke. Some headed for the roof hoping for a helicopter rescue only to find the doors to the roof locked. Trapped, many turned to prayer.

Steven Tall, Fiduciary's chief technology officer, was driving from his home in the New Jersey suburbs to work when he looked up and saw the north tower burning. Immediately, he called Comdisco, the company that operated Fiduciary's disaster recovery site in New Jersey. While employees there began unboxing desktop computers and attaching data lines, Tall drove home to grab two briefing books with the phone numbers of key staff and information technology contractors and instructions for recovering the company's data.

While Tall was en route, and nearly an hour after United's Flight 175 had plunged into the building, the south tower of the World Trade Center collapsed, killing everyone who remained inside. No one knew how many of Fiduciary's employees had escaped.

Normally, Henry Johnson, Fiduciary's head of Business Development (no relation to Charlie Johnson), would have been at work in the World Trade Center, but that day he was in Monterey, California, attending a conference. His wife called from New Jersey and said, "Turn on the TV." When he did, he saw the image of the burning Trade Center. Later,

Henry Johnson directed his wife to an emergency backup copy of the company's client list that was hidden in the basement of their home. The spouse of a Fiduciary employee picked up the list and drove it to Comdisco.

Like Henry Johnson, Jenny Bolt woke to the phone ringing. From London, Shelly Painter, Franklin Templeton's chief administrative officer for international business, was on the line. "A plane has crashed into the World Trade Center," she said. "What building is Fiduciary in?" As soon as she could dress, Jenny left for the office down the hill in San Mateo. Donna Ikeda got a similar call and quickly mobilized Human Resources staff throughout the company. Lorraine Mariano, the Human Resources director in Florida, was at the airport in New York. She had spent the day before meeting with staff at Fiduciary and was headed home when the news spread through the airport.

A conference room in San Mateo was turned into a central command room with situation updates posted as they came in. Conference calls were held every hour to connect Franklin and Fiduciary's management teams, which were scattered at locations around the world. A training room was converted into an employee call center. Within a couple of days, similar operations were established in Rancho Cordova and St. Petersburg to provide support, information and guidance for all Fiduciary employees and their families. As senior executives gathered to assess the situation, they were in touch with Fiduciary's president, Bill Yun. Yun had arrived at the World Trade Center earlier that morning, dropped off his bags for a business trip to Geneva later that day, and then left for New Jersey with a client. They were on the road when the first plane hit the north tower. He immediately headed for the disaster recovery site.

When Henry Johnson arrived in San Mateo after driving north from Monterey, Franklin's senior staff told him, "This is Fiduciary's meeting." "We debated whether we should call employees' home numbers," Jenny recalls. "There was an initial thought that we shouldn't do that, but Henry and I looked at each other and said, 'We've got to call.'" Lists of employees and their contact numbers were printed out. Other people began working to identify Franklin Templeton employees who were visiting Fiduciary on that day. The makeshift call center was staffed by people from throughout the company. People dropped what they were doing to undertake this difficult task. The effort went on all day and well into the night. Some of the calls were heartbreaking. A child asked, "Do you know where my mommy is?" In Florida, employees from technology and operations volunteered to drive to New Jersey to help. They drove overnight and then stayed for weeks to help in the recovery.

⤚Within eight hours of the attack, Fiduciary had a web page up reassuring customers that the company was still in business. Employees logging onto the site could find a number to call to give Franklin Templeton and Fiduciary an update on their whereabouts and situation. One of Franklin Templeton's eBusiness staff members found some freeware for a message board posting. Immediately, the stories and the queries flowed in. "Have you seen so-and-so. Do you know if she made it?"

⤚An executive team also worked to reassure the company's clients. "You had people thinking, 'All my savings are sitting with this company that doesn't exist, and I can't call them,'" says Jenny. Some clients did get through, however. At the recovery site, Yun fielded calls from clients who wanted to help. A representative from a foundation with $50 million invested with Fiduciary called to see if the people who handled the account were okay. Another client with $110 million invested offered office space. As *Forbes* quoted Yun, "Clients were calling us just to hear the sound of our voices and to offer condolences."

⤚A week after the attacks, Marty Flanagan and Jenny Bolt flew to New York to visit Fiduciary's temporary headquarters at Comdisco. They sat with Anne Tatlock as she talked with various families of employees who had died in the attack. "She was strong," Flanagan remembers, "but after one family left we could see the strain." Jenny reached out to her.

⤚Management recognized that the survival of the company and the emotional needs of employees demanded that Fiduciary move quickly to get back in business, but the company needed a new home, and dozens of other companies were suddenly in the same situation. Greg Johnson, who had been scheduled to fly to New York for a meeting on September 12 and to return on United Flight 93 from Newark, also worked to help Fiduciary get back on its feet. He called a friend who put him in touch with a firm that owned major properties in Manhattan. Soon, Fiduciary's surviving employees were working from folding tables and chairs in their new home at Rockefeller Plaza.

Altogether, 87 employees and 10 business partners associated with Fiduciary lost their lives on September 11. The deaths cut across virtually every department and represented a tremendous diversity of talent, tenure, age, job titles, cultures and faith. The lives lost included the company's general counsel, head of Human Resources, head of Investor Services, and treasurer. Senior portfolio managers, research analysts, custody officers, senior traders and the senior technology team, along with other employees, also perished. Some individuals had worked for the firm for almost 40 years, and one individual for less than a week. The loss of experience, knowledge and insight was far-reaching.

To provide some financial assistance to the families, the company established the FT Fiduciary Trust Memorial Fund. Less than five weeks after the attack, the company held a memorial service at the Cathedral of St. John the Divine. Anne Tatlock spoke, as did Tom Kean, the former governor of New Jersey and a member of Fiduciary's Board of Directors (Kean would later co-chair the 9/11 Commission). Yun then introduced the candle-lighting ceremony that followed. Prayers were offered from Jewish, Christian and Muslim traditions, only partially representing the broad spectrum of ethnic and religious backgrounds that had nourished the spiritual lives of those who had died in the attack.

In the aftermath of 9/11, many people were humbled by the small twists of fate that separated the survivors from those who had lost their lives. The story of Fiduciary's survival as a company was just as remarkable. The disaster planning that had been honed following the 1993 attack on the World Trade Center played a critical part in bringing

systems back on line quickly. Although many of Fiduciary's top managers lost their lives, an unusual number of them had been out of the office that day, forcing the cancellation of the executive team meeting that would normally have taken place that morning. The acquisition of Fiduciary by Franklin Templeton just months earlier provided a critical support system for locating and helping employees, reassuring investors and financing recovery.

⟞ Long after the events of the fall of 2001, Greg commented, "Looking back, one of the things that continues to resonate in my mind from that day and the days that followed is the way that our employees around the world and especially in New York City responded, how we helped each other through that very difficult time. It was an unforgettable display of humanity." Indeed, in an instant on September 11, the attacks had made Franklin Templeton and Fiduciary one family and one company.

To commemorate those who died in the attack on the World Trade Center, Fiduciary Trust commissioned this mural by artist Daniel Kohn. *Looking South* depicts the view from Fiduciary's former offices in the south tower.

September 11, 2001

At the memorial service held at New York's Cathedral of St. John the Divine, prayers were offered from a variety of religious traditions. Each employee and colleague lost in the September 11 attack was remembered by name. For many of the survivors, the service was a turning point in the long process of grieving and healing.

In Remembrance

Edelmiro Abad

Mukul Agarwala

Tariq Ammanullah

Wally Baran

Manette Marie Beckles

Shimmy D. Biegeleisen

Rita Blau

Sherry A. Bordeaux

Ronald M. Breitweiser

Kathleen A. Burns

Swarna Chalasani

Pete Checo

Robert Chin

Benjamin Keefe Clark

Anne Marie Martino-Cramer

Christopher Seton Cramer

Kenneth John Cubas

Patrick W. Danahy

Emy de La Peña

Jayceryll Malabuyoc de Chavez

Carol Keyes Demitz

Judy B. Diaz-Sierra

Michael D. Diehl

Edgar H. Emery, Jr.

Ruben Esquilin, Jr.

Bennett Lawson Fisher

Thomas J. Fisher

Ryan D. Fitzgerald

Eileen Flecha

David Fodor

Boyd A. Gatton

Alayne Friedenreich Gentul

Susan M. Getzendanner

Brian F. Goldberg

Dennis James Gomes

Sebastian Gorki

Joan Donna Griffith

Babita Girgamatie Guman

Felicia Hamilton

John Patrick Hart

John Clinton Hartz

Michelle Marie Henrique

Louis Steven Inghilterra

Jason K. Jacobs

Michael G. Jacobs

Alan K. Jensen

Brian Jones	Gloria Nieves
Stephen Joseph	Ivan Antonio Perez
Jane Josiah	Joseph O. Pick
Ruth Ellen Ketler	Wanda I. Prince
Nauka Kushitani	Carmen Rivera
Michele B. Lanza	Paul V. Rizza
Anna Laverty	Joshua A. Rosenthal
Alexis Leduc	Jason E. Sabbag
David S. Lee	Sita Sewnarine
Arnold Arboleda Lim	Nasima H. Simjee
Lorraine Lisi	Eric Smith
George Lopez	Klaus J. Sprockamp
Lee Charles Ludwig	Dick Stadelberger
James Maounis	Goumi Thackurdeen
Lester Marino	Thomas Tong
Joey Martinez	Doris S. Torres
Robert D. Mattson	Karamo Trerra
Brendan F. McCabe	Edward Raymond Vanacore
Barry J. McKeon	Arcangel Vazquez
Edmund McNally	Anthony M. Ventura
Mary Patricia Melendez	Todd Christopher Weaver
George L. Merino	Crossley R. Williams, Jr.
Ronald Milstein	Rodney James Wotton
Kleber R. Molina	Matthew David Yarnell
Krishna V. Moorthy	Igor Zukelman
Abner Morales	

CHAPTER
VIII

Struggle and Recovery

Marty Flanagan and Greg Johnson became co-presidents of Franklin Templeton in the fall of 2002. As the United States and the global economy adjusted to the collapse of the dot-com market and the war on terrorism, Franklin Templeton's employees found new ways to serve investors around the world.

Opposite: Franklin Templeton's global head-quarters in San Mateo, California.

Struggle and Recovery

Well done is better than well said.

— BENJAMIN FRANKLIN

As Charlie Johnson wrote to shareholders early in 2002, "An already difficult year for financial markets was exacerbated by the events of September 11." Franklin felt this downturn in the economy in a 16 percent decrease in earnings as net income fell from $562.1 million to $484.7 million. The global market decline reduced the value of assets under management, but this decline was not readily apparent. With the addition of Fiduciary's assets, Franklin's overall total AUM rose to $246.6 billion at the end of September 2001.

Many companies suffered in the aftermath of the market crash and the 9/11 attacks. In a conference call, Marty Flanagan and Greg Johnson announced that the company had become "very focused on cost containment." They outlined various cost-cutting strategies the company was already implementing. These included reducing advertising and promotion costs, moving back-office operations for Fiduciary from New York to Florida, and instituting salary reductions. The cuts were prudent, but not as drastic as they might have been, coming on the heels of Franklin Templeton's previous cost containment initiatives in 1998 and 1999. The speed with which the company was able to cut expenses reflected lessons learned in the earlier crisis. In fact, by the spring of 2002, the company was able to restore salaries for about two-thirds of the employees who had received pay cuts the previous fall.

⟨Having grimly managed tragedies and various business challenges during 2001 and the first half of 2002, Franklin was relieved in October 2002 when *Barron's* published an article that succinctly articulated Franklin's core strengths. The headline read: "Value in Vogue: Widely criticized in the late 1990s, Franklin Resources is back in style." The article quoted Charlie Johnson announcing that "we have been in positive sales all year long, including August when a lot of people weren't." It also noted how the company restructuring, which included stock buybacks and aggressive cost-cutting, was starting to bear fruit. Furthermore, the successful consolidation of the Franklin, Templeton and Mutual Series transfer agent systems was highlighted as an especially impressive accomplishment.

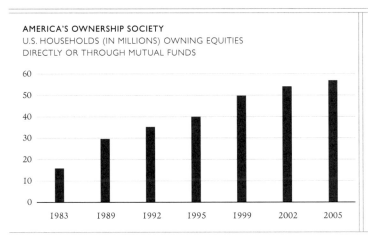

AMERICA'S OWNERSHIP SOCIETY
U.S. HOUSEHOLDS (IN MILLIONS) OWNING EQUITIES
DIRECTLY OR THROUGH MUTUAL FUNDS

From 1983 to 2005, the number of American households that owned stocks or mutual funds rose dramatically, topping 50 million by 2002.

International equities rode a roller coaster in the late 1990s and early years of the new century, but underlying changes held out promise for the future. After a few years of retrenchment in the Indian stock market, for example, with improved marketing and distribution and expanded investor education, the fund industry in India began to take off again in late 1998. More favorable government policies helped spur this rebirth. For the first time, in 1998, Indian regulators authorized mutual funds to invest overseas so they could diversify their holdings beyond the Indian equities market. The industry was given a further boost in 1999 from new tax incentives specifically targeted to fund shareholders. By the end of 1999, the *Financial Times* declared that "a mutual fund revolution inspired by the example of the U.S. is sweeping through India, transforming markets in its wake."

⁀As the industry grew, Charlie's patience with Franklin Templeton's work in India began to pay off. "He gave time and encouragement to people," says Vijay Advani. "He never demoralized people. He encouraged incremental progress. He was always looking to the long term."

In Mumbai, Franklin Templeton employees celebrated Family Day in February 2006. The Hawaiian-themed gathering included food, games and prizes.

Private sector funds were growing especially fast, "swiftly emerging from the shadow of the once dominant public sector fund managers." Franklin Templeton shared in this success, expanding to become the sixth-largest private mutual fund in India. One sign of the company's growing confidence in India was the launch of the first fund under the Franklin name outside of the United States. Called Franklin India Growth Fund, it focused on stocks with strong potential earnings growth, in contrast to Templeton India Growth Fund, which followed John Templeton's classic, disciplined value approach to picking stocks.

The financial crisis in Asia in 1998 had also created investment opportunities. In July 2000, Advani flew to Korea to negotiate the purchase of the remaining minority shares of the Korean asset management company in which Franklin Templeton owned a partial interest. The negotiations were difficult and dragged on for a month, with Advani shuttling back and forth between Korea and Singapore. Finally, he got the deal completed, and Franklin Templeton became a full owner of a new Korean subsidiary.

Expansion in India and Korea paralleled developments in other parts of the globe. By the fall of 2001, Franklin Templeton had distribution programs operating in 128 countries, with a representative in Beijing and a new sales office in Abu Dhabi. The 9/11 attacks, however, made global financial markets uneasy and posed a challenge to Franklin Templeton's leaders to find the right balance for the new millennium.

CHANGES AND CONTINUITY IN LEADERSHIP

Franklin Templeton's challenges in the early part of the new century continued. On the night of September 28, 2002, Chuck Johnson was involved in a domestic violence incident with his wife and was charged with assault. Faced with these charges, Chuck took a leave of absence, and nine months later pleaded no contest to the charges. He told the court, "There is no excuse for my actions in any way, and I make none. I take full responsibility." In a letter to the company's employees, he apologized for his conduct. The time away from the business had given him time to rethink his career. Rather than return to Franklin, in 2003 Chuck decided to pursue his own entrepreneurial dreams by forming Tano Capital, a private equity boutique focused on making direct investments in India and China.

Chuck's departure led to a restructuring of the executive team. Months earlier Al Gula had taken a leave of absence because of his wife's health. Although Gula continued as a consultant for some time, he eventually decided not to return to the business. Marty Flanagan and Greg became co-presidents of the company. The following spring, Jenny Bolt assumed the duties of chief information officer, and Jim Baio was appointed senior vice president and chief financial officer. Just as Franklin Templeton focused on reassuring employees and investors, the company got caught up in a larger controversy that had its roots in the dot-com boom years of the 1990s.

SEC INVESTIGATIONS

In the early 2000s, as the mutual fund industry suffered under the worst bear market since the 1970s, insiders also grew increasingly concerned about another trend hurting the industry: market timers. Fund managers generally seek to discourage shareholders from frequently trading in and out of funds as a way to chase the highest possible return. Market timing of this sort can cause sudden surges in fund redemptions that might force a manager to prematurely sell off portfolio holdings. This practice can increase the fund's trading costs and can also result in potentially higher capital gains or losses, which can hurt returns for long-term shareholders. As a result, while market timing was not illegal, many fund prospectuses contained clear language restricting or forbidding this practice.

While small-time market timers could be a nuisance, in the late 1990s and early 2000s the fund industry as a whole grew more concerned about aggressive, professional market timers. These sophisticated investors sought to profit from the fact that under standard mutual fund industry practice, fund net asset values (NAV) were calculated after the U.S. markets closed. As a result, the NAV of a fund didn't always reflect the actual value of that fund's portfolio investments, particularly those traded on markets in other parts of the world. Savvy market timers could use this situation to make quick profits through clever market timing strategies. These big-time market timers could have a negative impact on a fund, yet they were difficult to stop.

⏤In response to signs of increased market timing after 2000, a number of fund companies devised stricter measures to try to thwart market timers. Franklin Templeton was one of the earliest fund companies to establish such policies. In late 2000, some of the company's mutual fund boards determined that the funds would no longer accept new money from market timers and adopted other policies intended to curtail harmful market timing activity. The company also set up a "market timing desk" to review all transactions made by frequent fund traders. Finally, Franklin Templeton considered instituting redemption fees on its funds. Peter Jones, the president of Franklin Templeton Distributors, told Morningstar that "we prefer not to go the redemption-fee route because it reduces flexibility for investors who are not timers . . . but we will go that route if we conclude that it is the best route for all shareholders." By proposing such measures, Franklin Templeton and other fund companies were partly trying to encourage the SEC to provide clear guidance on how the fund industry should handle market timing. As Brian Lorenz, an outside counsel to the independent directors at Franklin Templeton funds, puts it, companies were asking the SEC at the time, "How do we restrict these people?"

⏤For its part, the SEC seemed to adopt a different point of view on the market timing issue. According to the SEC, the Investment Company Act of 1940 required all open-end funds to provide investors easy and regular access to their funds. "The SEC's position was that the shareholder's right to redeem their shares should be protected and shareholders should be able to go in and out [of their funds]," says Lorenz. The Commission believed that placing onerous restrictions or penalties on investors seeking to redeem shares was a violation of the rules under the 1940 Act. On the other hand, the SEC agreed that mutual fund companies ought to protect the majority of shareholders, who were long-term investors, from the risks posed by market timers.

⁓While the industry sought guidance on market timing issues, bigger issues occupied the SEC's attention following the collapse of the 1990s' stock bubble and the events of 9/11. Investors were increasingly angry about the evidence of high-level malfeasance by some in the investment industry. The potential conflict of interest between stock analysts and the investment banks that employed them was one issue that grabbed headlines. Even worse was the shocking demise of Enron and WorldCom, two prominent companies that suddenly collapsed after years of fraudulent accounting.

⁓As a response to these scandals, Congress passed the Sarbanes-Oxley Act (SOX), which President George W. Bush signed in July 2002. SOX tightened the regulations over corporate accounting and created structures designed to ensure ethical financial practices in publicly held companies. Most notably, it required CEOs and CFOs to certify the accuracy of their financial statements or risk going to jail. The SEC soon followed with new rules that applied the provisions of SOX to the mutual fund industry.

⁓Despite all the media attention to corporate scandals, the mutual fund industry remained relatively unscathed until late 2003. When a reporter for *Financial Planning* magazine asked Greg Johnson why this was so, he pointed to statistics that showed while "20 percent of stocks lost 60 percent or more of their value, not even one-tenth of one percent of all funds had the same type of loss." He also highlighted the industry's traditional emphasis on "putting the investor first" and the "strong regulatory framework between the SEC, NASD and 1940 Act."

⁓Greg and other executives also pointed out that Franklin Templeton, in particular, was already implementing many of the types of policies that Sarbanes-Oxley required as a result of the acquisition of Fiduciary Trust. According to Les Kratter, the Fiduciary deal led banking regulators to push "Franklin in areas where Franklin might not have moved as quickly in terms of business continuity, risk management and tighter processes. What it ultimately did for us is give us a leg up on compliance with Sarbanes-Oxley...because we already had the processes in place to do it. It forced a level of formality on our decision-making processes that was actually a good thing."

In the end, though, the mutual fund industry did not escape the avalanche of public criticism sparked by Enron and WorldCom. On September 3, 2003, Attorney General of New York Eliot Spitzer announced that a New York hedge fund, Canary Capital Partners, had been charged with working with a number of prominent fund companies to engage in illegal and/or improper trading activities. In return, the funds received, as one article phrased it, "payments and other inducements." Spitzer soon moved against a number of other firms. By early 2004, a total of 18 prominent fund companies were facing charges ranging from allowing minimal market timing to making deals to permit illegal late trading.

As one of the most prominent fund companies in the United States, Franklin Templeton was inevitably included in the various government investigations. In November 2003, the company disclosed that it had received requests for documents from the SEC, the New York Attorney General's Office and the Massachusetts Attorney General's Office. Eventually, Franklin Templeton was charged with allowing market timing and, in a separate action, with permitting insufficiently disclosed "directed brokerage" agreements (in other words, directing trades in fund portfolio securities to brokers who distributed Franklin Templeton funds). Franklin Templeton was not charged with any involvement in late trading. Morningstar, in its analysis of the cases against Franklin Templeton, concluded that while the government charges may "sully the record of what has been a reputable and responsible fund family," overall "[Franklin Templeton's] transgressions do not seem to rise to the level of malfeasance that we have seen at other firms." Nevertheless, these regulatory issues created a cloud of uncertainty.

Charlie responded to these charges with a laser-like focus. Nearly every day for months, he supervised a meeting of senior executives at 9 a.m. to discuss updates on the regulatory issues and ensure that everything was being done to meet the information needs of the investigators. The situation was particularly frustrating at the end of 2003, because Franklin Templeton was once again growing rapidly in a number of key strategic areas.

CONTINUED GLOBAL EXPANSION

For Franklin Templeton, the promise of the new century lay in global markets. By 2003 expansion in Asia, Latin America and Europe had begun to fuel the company's growth rate. Between 2002 and 2004, assets under management for customers in these parts of the world more than tripled, rising from roughly $21 billion to more than $70 billion in the space of two years. As a result of this increase, Franklin Templeton's assets under management held by investors outside the United States rose from 15 percent in 2002 to 27 percent by 2004.

Franklin Templeton stimulated this growth abroad by investing in technology. Despite the consolidation of its domestic shareholder services system in 1998, the company had continued to operate on a variety of systems abroad. In 2003 the company began to implement a single

Mark Mobius shares the stage with David Chang, senior director from the Hong Kong office, as a dragon parade crosses behind them. The event celebrated Chinese New Year and the kickoff of the Franklin Templeton Asian Growth campaign in March 2004.

global trading structure and image workflow system. The challenge, according to Basil Fox, was to implement global service standards and integrate data systems while maintaining the company's ability to respond to the needs of local or regional markets for specific services or products. Fox oversaw an organizational integration of the company's formerly segregated U.S. and international transfer agencies to form a single global transfer agency. The company also internationalized more of its processing operations. For example, in India, Franklin expanded the number of employees who were involved in account reconciliation and processing.

⏎This global integration helped fuel growth in many of the company's major international markets. In India, Franklin Templeton had grown to become one of the largest private mutual fund operations in the country. Franklin Templeton's success in India resulted from strategies similar to those that led to the company's growth in the United States: a loyal distribution network and a steady, value-oriented approach to investing that avoided speculative bets. In India, the company offered a wide variety of fund options to satisfy diverse investor interests, and introduced innovative new products that included the first "fund of funds" in the country, the first floating-rate income fund, the first "infotech fund"

For the *2004 Annual Report*, the four members of the Office of the Chairman posed in the global headquarters in San Mateo. (L-R): Vice Chairman Rupert H. Johnson, Jr., Vice Chairman Anne M. Tatlock, Chairman Charles B. Johnson and Vice Chairman Harmon E. Burns.

BUILDING RELATIONSHIPS IN JAPAN

After opening an office in Tokyo in 1996, Franklin Templeton struggled to find a foothold in the Japanese market. Entry into this market was difficult for foreign financial firms, due to the close connections between asset management companies and their affiliated brokerage firms.

Then in 1997, the failure of a number of leading companies, including Japan's oldest and fourth-largest brokerage, Yamaichi Securities Co., created an opportunity. For years, Franklin had tried to recruit Kozo Matsumoto, president of Yamaichi Asset Management in New York. Matsumoto had worked with various Franklin executives since the late 1980s on mortgage-backed securities accounts. After Yamaichi went bankrupt, he agreed to join the Franklin team.

With Matsumoto on board, Franklin finally was able to recruit a high-caliber, all-Japanese team with relationships with institutional investors. The firm scored a coup when portfolio manager Toru Ohara agreed to leave Tokyo Marine to join Franklin Templeton, and sales increased dramatically when Shin-Ichi Furukawa came on board. By 2006 assets under management in Japan topped $4 billion.

and the first private pension plan. Franklin Templeton's growth in India was also propelled by a merger with Pioneer ITI, an Indian fund company established in 1993. At a cost of $50 million, the acquisition brought the total number of accounts up to 900,000 and doubled assets under management to $1.8 billion.

Meanwhile Franklin Templeton continued to build on its base around the world. In Korea, the company had nearly $3 billion in assets under management by the end of 2003, and had become one of the larger foreign asset managers in the country. Assets under management in Japan surged as well, from $510 million to $2.19 billion. In Canada, Franklin Templeton's continuing success was evident when the DALBAR rating agency ranked Franklin Templeton's French and English call center operations number one and number two, respectively, for service excellence. A leading German independent financial advisor magazine, *Performance,* named Franklin Templeton the investment company with the best-performing mutual funds, the best brand and the best relationships with financial professionals. These direct expansions of the business in global markets and evidence of customer satisfaction sustained Franklin Templeton's growth. At the same time, Franklin expanded its range of investment products for an increasingly diverse customer base both at home and abroad. The growth of these international products and markets continued to strengthen Franklin Templeton's hand when it came to institutional investors.

A GLOBAL INSTITUTIONAL PLATFORM

Franklin's progress was not just the result of international economics, but of decisions to combine companies and bring highly qualified executives onto the same playing field. Marty Flanagan's relocation to California after the Templeton acquisition had set the stage for the cultural and strategic integration of Franklin and Templeton. Bill Yun's move in February 2002 aimed to achieve a similar objective for Franklin and Fiduciary. In February, Franklin Templeton announced that Yun would lead a new organization called FTI Institutional (now known as Franklin Templeton Institutional). By combining the investment expertise of Franklin Templeton with Fiduciary's long experience with high net-worth and institutional clients, Franklin Templeton hoped this new organization would accelerate the growth of its institutional business.

⟿ The new FTI Institutional offered the investment expertise of Franklin, Templeton and Fiduciary under the umbrella of a global business development and management platform with offices in the United States,

Kozo Matsumoto (front row, third from left), the head of Franklin Templeton's group in Japan, and Charlie Johnson (front row, fourth from left) with the staff in Franklin Templeton's Tokyo office in April 2004.

Hong Kong, London, Melbourne, Tokyo and Toronto. Headquartered in New York, the team focused on a broad array of institutional clients that included government and corporate pension plans, foundations and endowments. Yun asserted that the new organization would allow Franklin Templeton to offer "a full spectrum" of over 30 investment strategies and a presence in 29 countries.

⮞Franklin Templeton saw several opportunities in the changing institutional market. Years earlier, this industry sector had been dominated by trust companies and insurance companies. It was a sleepy business, and investors "were mainly concerned about relative performance." In the low-return environment that followed the end of the dot-com bubble, however, institutional investors faced other pressures. Over half of all U.S. pension plans described themselves as underfunded, and many pension plans in European Union countries were in a similar situation. Increasingly, institutional investors focused on absolute returns and employed more sophisticated investment strategies. Many were looking for opportunities to broaden their investments into global public and private markets to provide more stable returns. As some developing nations began to relax government restrictions on domestic institutions, allowing them to invest outside the country, the number of institutional investors in this sector increased as well. All of these changes in the marketplace created opportunities. They also created a need for added capacity.

⮞In their search for growth opportunities, institutional investors looked increasingly to earlier-stage companies that were still in the entrepreneurial mode. Franklin Templeton's global network of offices supported research in emerging markets, and this capacity expanded when the company made another strategic acquisition in 2003.

ACQUIRING DARBY

As far back as the early 1990s, Franklin's institutional clients had sought greater opportunities to invest in private equity placements in emerging markets. To meet that demand, in 1994 Franklin took advantage of an unusual opportunity to help launch a new emerging markets investment group known as Darby Overseas Investments, Ltd.

⌁Darby was the brainchild of former U.S. Secretary of the Treasury Nicholas Brady. Aiming to invest in emerging markets, particularly in Latin America, Darby attracted significant investment from companies headquartered in the San Francisco Bay Area, including Bechtel Corporation and Franklin Resources. Brady joined the fund boards of various Templeton funds, including Templeton Emerging Markets Investment Trust (TEMIT), in 1994. That same year, Franklin became one of the original investors in Darby, taking a 12.7 percent equity stake. Working together, Charlie Johnson and Nicholas Brady realized that they shared a vision of the coming prosperity of the developing world.

⌁Darby's strategy involved investing growth capital in privately held companies in sectors such as manufacturing, consumer products, banking and telecommunications. The original plan focused on bringing the U.S. style of private equity investing to the emerging markets, incubating these businesses until they were ready for an initial public offering, at which point Darby could liquidate its equity. After a few short years, however, the partners realized

DARBY
OVERSEAS
INVESTMENTS

Darby Overseas Investments was founded by former U.S. Secretary of the Treasury Nicholas F. Brady. Recruited by President Reagan in late 1988, Brady served as Secretary of the Treasury throughout the entire George Bush presidency and made the Latin American debt crisis a key focus of his tenure. The insights gained and relationships forged through successful negotiation of the $148 billion Latin American debt restructuring led Brady to develop and launch Darby Overseas Investments shortly after leaving public service in 1993.

Initially limiting the firm's private equity investing to Latin America, Darby has since expanded its business to emerging markets throughout the world. In the past 10 years, Darby's cumulative committed capital has grown from $148 million to $2 billion, with Darby-managed private equity and mezzanine funds putting money to work in Latin American, Asia, and central and eastern Europe.

that development in these markets moved more slowly than they had anticipated. Recognizing a need to change the strategy and bring in management for the long haul, Brady called Richard Frank.

After a 26-year career in developing markets, Frank had risen to become managing director and interim president of the World Bank. He listened carefully as Brady expressed his frustration with Darby's slow progress. When Brady asked if he would consider leaving the bank to become CEO of Darby, Frank decided to pursue the opportunity.

Soon after his arrival at Darby in July 1997, Frank realized that Darby's staff did not have the right mix of skills for the strategy the company wanted to pursue. He recruited a number of veterans from the International Finance Corporation. At the time, Darby was suffering, not from inherently bad investments, but from exposure to changes taking place in the currency markets as a number of Latin American countries moved from fixed to floating rates with severe devaluation. A number of investments had to be written off. Through this transition, Frank benefited from a board of directors that understood volatility in international markets. "It was a very down-to-earth board," he says. Among them, Charlie Johnson listened and was patient. "He was watching us take the firm through this transition as we tried to raise capital and get traction."

As Darby turned the corner in the late 1990s, Franklin Resources increased its investment in the firm and its subsidiary operations. In 2001 Franklin joined with IBM, Comcast Interactive Capital, Bechtel and other partners to create Darby Technology Ventures. When Darby redeemed Chemical Bank's equity stake, Franklin decided to increase its interest. "That was a real endorsement," says Frank. But the company needed more capital to take advantage of the opportunities it was seeing to invest. "We talked to a large pension fund and to an insurance company," Frank recalls. Then Charlie told Nicholas Brady that Franklin might be interested in acquiring Darby. Following negotiations, in August 2003 Franklin Templeton announced that it would buy the Darby shares that it did not own for approximately $75.9 million.

As with past acquisitions, Franklin Templeton stuck to its philosophy of letting people do what they do best. The company stepped in to integrate Darby's back-office operations, but left Richard Frank and his team to continue managing the investment side of the business. Darby employees enjoyed the benefits and resources that Franklin Templeton made available to its people. "Some people were afraid that we would be swallowed up in a big bureaucracy," Frank says, "but that didn't materialize." By becoming part of the Franklin Templeton family, Darby gained access to a much larger base of investors. Franklin Templeton gained a partner with its ear to the ground in many parts of the world and a firm that could offer its own clients different types of funds in the critical alternative asset category.

The combination fueled Franklin's growing success. By the fall of 2003, global expansion, the turnaround in the U.S. market and the resurgence of Franklin Templeton were in full evidence. Total assets under management had risen to nearly $302 billion, compared to $247.8 billion the year before. Having learned again the lessons of boom and bust, the company kept its focus on cost control even as it continued to expand. In 2003, for example, employee headcount declined from roughly 6,700 to about 6,500. All of these developments gave Charlie confidence and paved the way for the next step in the transition to a new generation of leaders.

GLOBAL EXPANSION
FRANKLIN TEMPLETON'S ASSETS UNDER MANAGEMENT
(IN BILLIONS), 1998–2004

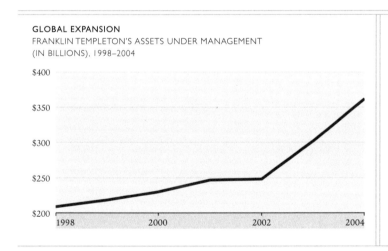

Despite turbulence in the financial markets between 1998 and 2002, Franklin Templeton's assets under management (AUM) continued to grow. In 2002 AUM began a dramatic climb, from approximately $250 billion to more than $350 billion by 2004.

By late 2003, two internal contenders remained for the CEO position at Franklin: Marty Flanagan and Greg Johnson. To Charlie and the employees who worked for them, these two men were remarkably compatible, and for Charlie the need to move the succession process along was clear. He announced that at the beginning of 2004, Marty and Greg would become co-CEOs, sharing responsibility for strategy and day-to-day operations. Charlie would continue as chairman of the board.

Management theorists often discourage the idea of co-CEOs, but for Marty and Greg the arrangement made sense given the company's situation and their personal lives. As Marty saw it, Greg had a stronger entrepreneurial background with experience in portfolio management, product creation, sales and marketing. Marty's strengths were in administration and finance, but he had been mentored in the world of investing by John Templeton. Both men had deep experience in all parts of the business.

With more than $300 billion in assets under management and 6,500 employees working on six continents, the travel schedule demanded by the job was daunting. Marty and Greg, both in their early forties, had young families, and sharing the job allowed them to be home a little more often. It also allowed them to cover more ground, speaking to investors, brokers, shareholders and others while visiting Franklin Templeton's offices around the world.

For this new leadership, resolving the regulatory issues was job one. Late in 2004, the company settled the charges related to directed brokerage and market timing filed by the SEC, as well as directed brokerage charges filed by the California Attorney General, without admitting or denying any wrongdoing. In addition, it agreed to make public the types and amounts of marketing support it made to fund distributors. Franklin had already voluntarily stopped directed brokerage a year earlier in 2003. Franklin also agreed to affirm that its traders were required to be impartial when choosing brokers to carry out trades, without any consideration of which brokers were the biggest promoters of Franklin Templeton funds.

To the company's credit, tensions over regulatory issues had hardly slowed the pace of innovation or expansion.

⟨From the time Greg Johnson and Marty Flanagan officially took the reins in January 2004, Franklin Templeton's performance was outstanding. The three pillars of Franklin Templeton's business—investment performance, customer service and marketing—had never been stronger, and results proved it. When the company closed its fiscal year in September 2004, net income was up nearly 41 percent while assets under management had risen from $301.9 billion to $361.9 billion. Over 95 percent of the company's U.S. long-term retail assets were in funds that were performing in the top two quartiles of their respective Lipper peer groups for three-, five- and ten-year periods. Meanwhile, the company was recognized in Korea, Switzerland, the UK, Germany, Austria, Taiwan and Canada as one of the best investment managers in the market. Surveys showed that investors ranked Franklin Templeton's website as one of the best in the financial

Franklin Templeton's brand advertising promotes diversification through its autonomous investment management groups—in this case, Franklin, Templeton and Mutual Series. This ad, which ran in *The Wall Street Journal*, was part of a series promoting the company's multi-manager offerings in the U.S.

services sector. In Germany, the United States, the UK and France, Franklin Templeton's shareholder services operations were ranked first, second or third by shareholders and financial advisors. This performance was remarkable given the scale of customer service operations—nearly 15 million accounts around the world. It also boded well for Franklin Templeton's strategic effort to create a global platform for shareholder services.

A GLOBAL PLATFORM, A GLOBAL IDENTITY

The acquisitions that helped expand Franklin Templeton's products and geographic reach also increased the complexity of the company's global operations and identity. As international markets had become increasingly important to Franklin Templeton's continued growth, so had the need to integrate marketing, products and operations on a global basis.

The effort to create a single global brand evolved from the fact that Franklin Templeton had become much more than a mutual fund company. Investment services at Franklin were offered through many vehicles in addition to the traditional mutual funds, including institutional accounts, corporate accounts and privately managed accounts for individuals. Together, these products and services shaped the scope and character of Franklin Templeton's business. As Greg told employees, "We have to change our thinking from a mutual fund company to an investment management organization." To communicate this fact to investors, Greg led an effort in 2000 to change the company's brand name to Franklin Templeton Investments. The new name, he said, reflected the "shift in corporate identity and culture."

With the adoption of the new brand name, Greg also created a global branding committee to communicate a new image of the company to investors and business partners around the world. Under the leadership of John Greer, the newly hired executive vice president of Marketing, the presentation of the brand changed in a number of ways over the next several years. In 2001 the Franklin Templeton Investments name was introduced globally, along with the Ben Franklin or "Ben Head" logo.

The Templeton marquee was changed to Franklin Templeton Investments in more than 20 countries.

⟩At home, Greer launched the company's first brand advertising campaign combining all three retail investment brands—Franklin, Templeton and Mutual Series—under the Franklin Templeton Investments banner in 2001. The campaign emphasized Franklin's unique multi-manager structure to help the company stand out among its competitors. "Through research, we found that very few financial advisors or investors had a complete understanding of what Franklin Templeton Investments had to offer. But when we presented them with the multi-manager concept, it resonated and increased their estimation of the firm," said Greer. As a result of this effort, Franklin Templeton's name recognition increased to the highest level in years. This multi-manager concept, sometimes expressed as "the expertise of many, the strength of one," became the basis for the company's positioning and was extended to other markets, channels and internal communications.

As part of its new global branding strategy, Franklin Templeton introduced the image of Benjamin Franklin to investors around the world. This ad, which ran in Italy, set the stage for specific product promotion in later years.

With the consolidation of global systems and marketing, Franklin Templeton also moved to integrate its business within particular product lines. The company's leaders recognized a need to restructure Mutual Series, and in 2005 Peter Langerman was recruited to lead this effort. Langerman had joined Mutual Series in 1986 and became CEO of the group in 1998 following Michael Price's retirement. In 2002 Langerman left Mutual and Franklin to serve as director of New Jersey's Division of Investment, overseeing employee pension funds. Upon returning to Franklin in 2005, Langerman and Bill Lippman launched a new organization, Franklin Value Group, as an umbrella for various Franklin and Mutual Series investments. With $50 billion in assets under management, this entity represented another important "value" component of the new global strategy. It also aligned two different generations of investment managers around one enduring set of organizational values and strategies.

As part of the effort to integrate the business within product lines, the company also created the Franklin Templeton Fixed Income Group in late 2005. Under the direction of Chris Molumphy, this new line of business

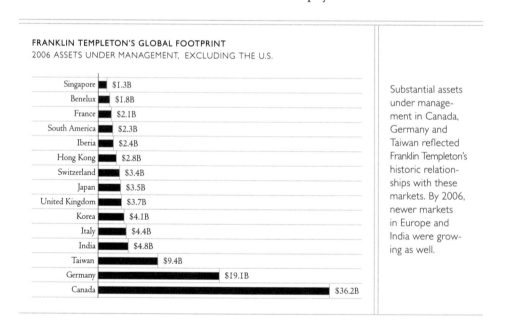

FRANKLIN TEMPLETON'S GLOBAL FOOTPRINT
2006 ASSETS UNDER MANAGEMENT, EXCLUDING THE U.S.

Singapore	$1.3B
Benelux	$1.8B
France	$2.1B
South America	$2.3B
Iberia	$2.4B
Hong Kong	$2.8B
Switzerland	$3.4B
Japan	$3.5B
United Kingdom	$3.7B
Korea	$4.1B
Italy	$4.4B
India	$4.8B
Taiwan	$9.4B
Germany	$19.1B
Canada	$36.2B

Substantial assets under management in Canada, Germany and Taiwan reflected Franklin Templeton's historic relationships with these markets. By 2006, newer markets in Europe and India were growing as well.

combined groups from Franklin and Fiduciary to provide a more coherent menu of products to customers looking for fixed income investments.

⬥ The global integration of the company's brand, products and operations in the early years of the new millennium reflected the coming of age of a new generation of leadership. Unfortunately, Franklin Templeton's growing success also attracted the attention of competitors.

A NEW ERA IN LEADERSHIP

Marty Flanagan and Greg Johnson worked well together, but as Charlie Johnson later said, one of the problems with the horse race concept was that it posed the risk that Franklin Templeton might eventually lose a very talented individual. Charlie took the perspective that while people are valued, no one person, including himself, is indispensable to the organization. In the mid-1990s, Greg discovered this when he went to his father with news that a headhunter had contacted him about becoming a national sales manager for another company. Charlie simply replied: "Sounds like a great job." Greg chose to stay with Franklin, but when the competition came calling for Marty Flanagan in 2005, Flanagan left to

Ed Jamieson, Greg Johnson and Jenny (Johnson) Bolt grew up in families with deep roots and experience in the mutual fund industry. In 2006 Ed Jamieson (left) served as president of Franklin Advisers, Inc., Greg Johnson as CEO of Franklin Templeton Investments and Jenny Bolt as Franklin Templeton's executive vice president for Operations and Technology.

become president and CEO of AMVESCAP, a leading independent global investment manager with roots in the United Kingdom.

With Marty's departure, Greg became sole CEO of Franklin Templeton. He had come a long way since beginning on the early morning shift at the trading desk in the 1980s. Greg had been developed in the same way that Charlie, Rupert and Harmon Burns had developed other promising executives, through hands-on experience in different parts of the business. He had managed investments, led the company's sales and marketing efforts, and become increasingly involved in strategy. As part of the executive team during the Templeton, Mutual Series and Fiduciary acquisitions, he had wrestled with the challenges of integrating organizations and creating a common culture. As co-CEO, he had forged his own leadership style while being part of a strong two-person team.

By nature, Greg emulated his father. He listened and delegated, trusting others to do what they do best. He could disarm people with a quiet sense of humor. In a small group, he was a careful listener to what others had to say. In front of a group as a speaker, he had an instinct for his audience and could connect with people from many different backgrounds. Organized and in command of the facts, he could be focused and zero in on what was important.

The modern-day demands on a CEO of a global company are enormous. As co-CEOs, Greg and Marty had shared work, travel and decision-making responsibilities; as sole CEO, Greg faced a heightened challenge to effectively manage the business while simultaneously traveling the world.

One of Greg's first priorities as CEO was to consolidate the structure of Franklin Templeton and align it with the company's increasingly global strategy. In the fall of 2005, he announced a new organizational structure that focused on functional elements and reduced his number of direct reports. The new structure, Greg told Franklin employees, "enables quick decision-making, allows groups to leverage core capabilities and resources, and broadens the opportunities available to all employees."

Greg addressed Franklin Templeton employees worldwide at a videoconferenced meeting later that year. In that address, he congratulated the team for stellar financial performance, noting that assets under management, gross sales and net sales were all up dramatically. Greg attributed that performance to three factors: "We continue to deliver very strong, consistent relative performance from our portfolio teams. Our sales and marketing groups continue to build relationships around the globe. And finally, we continue to deliver excellent service to our clients and customers."

Greg went on to outline the factors he believed would continue to propel Franklin Templeton's success: putting clients first; expanding the breadth of U.S. products; expanding local asset management companies and retail presence around the globe; and creating new alliances that would pave the way for thousands of new financial advisors to sell Franklin Templeton products. "Our mission, as you know, is to be the premier global investment management organization," he told employees that day, adding that "sometimes that's not easy. In a performance-based organization, sometimes it's difficult to weigh a metric versus those values that we have instilled within our company."

To sustain Franklin Templeton's competitive advantages in the marketplace, the company continued to innovate in 2005 and 2006. The

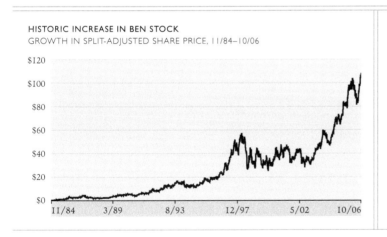

HISTORIC INCREASE IN BEN STOCK
GROWTH IN SPLIT-ADJUSTED SHARE PRICE, 11/84–10/06

Franklin stockholders who stayed with the company from 1984 to 2006 enjoyed a tremendous increase in the value of their stock. One dollar invested in BEN shares in November 1984 was worth more than $100 in October 2006.

new Franklin Global Real Estate Fund provided investors with income and growth by investing in a global portfolio of real estate investment trusts. The company also launched an Emerging Markets Small Cap Fund for U.S. investors. International growth continued with new offices opening in China, Brazil and Mexico, while traditional markets in Canada, Germany and Taiwan remained strong. By the middle of 2006, three out of 10 shareholders of Franklin Templeton funds lived outside the United States.

As it entered 2007, Franklin Templeton continued to deliver the rewards of persistence and perspective to investors and shareholders. The company's steadfast adherence to vision and values had helped assets under management climb from $2.5 million in 1957 to over $500 billion in 2006. On the eve of the company's 60th anniversary, approximately 8,000 employees dedicated to the investing needs of customers around the globe were transacting business in 15 different languages and 25 currencies. Together, these employees, like those who came before them, make Franklin Templeton one of the premier global investment management companies in the world.

Twenty years after Franklin's stock debuted as BEN on the New York Stock Exchange, CEO Greg Johnson, with colleagues and board members, stood at the podium in December 2006 to ring the closing bell.

Conclusion

Modern readers are often surprised to discover that Benjamin Franklin's *Autobiography* ends around 1757, long before Franklin emerged as one of the founding fathers of the United States.

⁓While clear in its articulation of his moral code, faults, aspirations and values, the *Autobiography* offers no insights into the events and issues that would shape the identity of a future nation. But that may be precisely the point: Following a consistent set of values and code of conduct can build a lasting legacy that far exceeds the standard measures of success.

⁓Benjamin Franklin's values have been central to the life and culture of Franklin Resources through six decades of change and growth. The company's corporate culture still reflects many of Benjamin Franklin's traits: appreciation for the diversity of human cultures and personalities, rigorous attention to self-improvement and financial discipline, attention to detail and service, and delight in the advantages of new technologies and ways of doing business. The company also shares Benjamin Franklin's fundamental enthusiasm for the future.

⁓In 1957 Charlie Johnson was an evangelist for the mutual fund idea. He believed that mutual funds offered ordinary people "access to the investment world unlike any other product up to that time." They were affordable and gave people who didn't have great wealth a way to invest in a diversified pool of stocks and bonds. Able to invest small amounts on a regular basis, these investors could benefit from professional management. Sixty years later, nearly half of all U.S. households own mutual funds, and a growing percentage of the world's investors have followed suit.

⌐Having survived the go-go years of the 1960s and the dot-com bubble of the 1990s, Franklin Templeton is less likely than many companies to fret about being out of favor through the inevitable cycles of boom and bust. Rather, the company has come to be characterized by the relentless and disciplined search for fundamental value as expressed through the investing philosophies of Charlie Johnson, Max Heine and Sir John Templeton, as well as the founders of Fiduciary, Bissett and Darby.

⌐As Franklin Templeton's past makes clear, successful investing is not just a matter of discipline, but of deep knowledge, intuition and integrity. "The art of investing will never go away," says Greg Johnson. "It makes our success dependent on good, smart people." Over the past 60 years, innovations in technology and the marketplace have led some to believe that with indexing and direct selling, there is little need for "art" in investing anymore and hardly a role for advice. Greg rejects this point of view. "There will always be a place for the human element. That's why we exist as an organization."

⌐Franklin Templeton's long commitment to integrity infuses both the advice it offers investors and its investment decisions. "We operate in a highly regulated environment," says Greg. "You can make rules all day long, but at the end of the day the ethical behavior of the company will depend on the strength of the values of its people."

⌐Global expansion challenges the idea of a common culture and set of values, but Franklin Templeton has been able to sustain a collective identity and sense of purpose even as it encourages diversity within its various business units. Throughout his career, Charlie gave individuals autonomy and expressed his confidence in their abilities, even when they made mistakes. Franklin Templeton's executives have likewise had to learn to balance the autonomy they give to portfolio managers, especially, with the need to create coherence within the organization's strategy and operations. This creative tension has infused the history of the company since 1947 and will no doubt shape its future.

⌐The continued role of the Johnson family is responsible, in large part, for the consistency of values that has shaped Franklin Templeton for 60 years. Through three generations the Johnsons have shared the leadership of Franklin Templeton with a host of talented executives and employees, and the presence of the family as major shareholders also adds value to the business. It takes the focus off short-term accomplishments or disappointments and sustains the sense that personal and family honor are at stake in every Franklin Templeton transaction. "There's a natural alignment," says Greg, "between the interests of the investor who is concerned with long-term performance and someone in my position who feels not only a responsibility to shareholders, customers and employees, but to the legacy of my father and grandfather as well."

In his letter to Benjamin Franklin in 1783, Benjamin Vaughn wrote: "Our sensations being very much fixed to the moment, we are apt to forget that more moments are to follow the first, and consequently that a man should arrange his conduct to suit the whole of a life." The same can be said about the history and the future of a company. Franklin Templeton's future will be framed by day-to-day decisions yet to be made. Each of those decisions will be rooted not only in modern-day norms and culture, but also in the experience and perspective gained over 60 years— and just as important, in the timeless Franklin Templeton values of hard work, integrity and persistence.

Acknowledgments

Over the course of 60 years, many people have shaped the history and success of Franklin Templeton Investments. Named or not within this history, their contributions have been significant and appreciated.

To capture this history, the authors reached out to current and former employees, as well as to many friends of the company. The following individuals graciously gave their time for face-to-face or telephone interviews: Vijay Advani, Penny Alexander, Sheila Amoroso, Harris Ashton, Milton Berlinski, Jennifer Bolt, Harmon Burns, Rafael Costas, Tom Cotter, Peter Cowie, Jeff Everett, Marty Flanagan, Joe Fortunato, Basil Fox, Richard Frank, John and Rosemary Galbraith, Deborah Gatzek, John Greer, Nancy Hessel, Donna Ikeda, Frank Isola, Harold Jacob, Ed Jamieson, Ann Johnson, Andrew Johnson, Charles B. Johnson, Chuck Johnson, Earl and Ann Johnson, Greg Johnson, Henry Johnson, Rupert H. Johnson, Jr., Peter Jones, Ken Koskella, Les Kratter, Peter Langerman, William Lippman, Brian Lorenz, Bruce MacGowan, Ed McVey, Clark Nielsen, Shelly Painter, Jerry Palmieri, Jed Plafker, Michael Price, Don Reed, Murray Simpson, Richard Stoker, Anne Tatlock, Tom Walsh, Hans Wisser, Lou Woodworth and Bill Yun.

Family members of past employees helped provide photos and information, including Elizabeth Bowers, Mark Grosvenor and Dr. Jack Templeton.

On many occasions Mary Gamba and Rose Kaufman in the offices of Charlie and Rupert Johnson took time to help us track down people or information.

On visits to various Franklin Templeton offices in North America, many people went out of their way to help us find historical materials. Thank you in particular to Hugh Cameron, Maurizio Chen, John McComb and Kevin Murakami in Toronto; Carol Fullart in St. Petersburg; Lisa Testa and Ann Margaret Ullrich in Fort Lauderdale; Carolyn Martini and Kelly Michael in Short Hills; Clark Hobbs in Rancho Cordova; and Helen Rutt in the Global Research Library.

At the Investment Company Institute (ICI) in Washington, D.C., Terry Brooks and Larry Maffia provided insight and helpful information on the history of the mutual fund industry.

Two other history professionals helped launch this project. Alison Moore assisted in organizing the Franklin Templeton Archives in San Mateo, while oral historian Marilyn Tobias conducted interviews with Charlie and Rupert Johnson, Harmon Burns, Bill Lippman and Dick Stoker.

Throughout the project we received assistance from Franklin Templeton's Global Marketing Division. John Greer and Virginia Marans commented on the manuscript. In Creative Services, Debra Steinholtz assisted with design and development of graphic material, and Paul Carnevale, Clifford Ng, Sue Sasano and Sue Wong provided critical project support. Cynthia Hanson, Barbara King, Alex Ling and Sue Oliver provided copyediting and proofreading that improved the manuscript through many iterations. Alan Huey designed charts and graphs for the book. Marci Roberts and Harold Wilkes helped with scans. Laura Komar helped gather photos from Franklin Templeton's international operations. Matt Dunn in Digital Solutions provided assistance for the taped interviews in San Mateo. In Print Production and Management, Michael Massette and Roxelle Paris provided expert guidance on printer selection and management.

As the book moved through various drafts, a number of people read and reread the manuscript. Their suggestions helped improve the flow and accuracy of the text. It was quite a time commitment, and we thank them all for their feedback.

The book would not have come together without the tremendous help we received from our partners in Franklin Templeton's Corporate Communications Department. Kudos to Harold Botts, Lisa Gallegos, Kristine Hurley, Vedrana Jagodic, Stacey Johnston, Jennifer Muñoz, Jayne Springer, Hellen Tam and Bill Weeks, with Jon Boilard and Holly Gibson Brady making up the internal core team that steered the project from beginning to end.

At Vantage Point, Jacqui Dietrich provided invaluable help with research and project management, Ernie Grafe created and maintained the image database, Craig Chapman prepared the raw transcripts from interviews, and Lois Facer facilitated the transcript management process. Clint Dietrich helped with videography. Patrick Romano dug through the business press. Liz Van Houten provided initial copyediting.

As editor and project manager, Marji Wilkens never lost sight of the story we were trying to tell, and offered valuable improvements to the manuscript every step of the way.

The book was designed by Raul Cabra of Cabra Diseño. Raul's grasp of the Franklin Templeton culture and personality led to an ageless design that enhances the text. We are grateful for Raul's keen eye and skills.

Above all, thanks to Charlie Johnson for providing the opportunity to tell the story of Franklin Templeton. Throughout the project he graciously shared his memories and exhibited the crucial judgment that has made Franklin Templeton a trusted name for millions of investors around the globe.

Endnotes

The following endnotes reference the sources for all direct quotes in the text from outside sources, joint interviews and telephone interviews conducted by the authors. All other quotes are taken from face-to-face interviews conducted by Eric John Abrahamson for the Franklin Templeton history project. Transcripts from these interviews are in the Franklin Templeton Archives. Quotes from Benjamin Franklin used to introduce each chapter come from *Quotations of Benjamin Franklin* (Bedford, MA: Applewood Books, 2003).

PAGE
NUMBER

(9) "Half the electric utilities raised their dividends every year...." Alyssa Lappen, "Reinventing Franklin," *Institutional Investor,* November 1, 1997.

(14) "...securities of companies deriving income from outside the United States." "Today's Offerings Exceed $25,000,000: New or Outstanding Stock in Four Concerns to Be Available in Market," *The New York Times,* November 9, 1954.

(16) "That was a judgment failure. We should have just bitten the bullet. But we didn't want the brokers to stop selling the funds...." Interview with Charles B. Johnson by Marilyn Tobias, July 26, 2005.

(18) "Charlie's philosophy was just the same as his father's. You work hard. You play by the rules. And you never

PAGE
NUMBER

quit, you persevere." Interview with Richard C. Stoker by Marilyn Tobias, September 13, 2005.

(19) "I was kind of preparing myself intellectually. I was just curious. I'd been around the business, and I just wanted to see it from the outside, from another person's perspective. I was verifying my own conclusions." Interview with Rupert H. Johnson, Jr., by Marilyn Tobias, July 28, 2005.

(20) "Everybody had to be a salesman in the organization." Ibid.

(20) "We tried to get their attention by not necessarily talking about products, but by trying to increase their productivity....We became a sounding board." Ibid.

(20) "You stopped everything you were doing, you had a calculator, and you took orders." Ibid.

(22) "…had plenty of money, and their wholesalers had unlimited expense accounts.…The key was to help them get new clients." Interview with Richard C. Stoker by Marilyn Tobias, September 13, 2005.

(22) "…owned the whole city and Long Island because they advertised the lion coming out of the subway.… They were teaching everybody about mutual funds. They trailblazed for everybody." Ibid.

(23) "At the top of 120 Broadway, I spent three weeks in one building going up and down and being thrown out by brokers on every floor. Then all of a sudden, maybe down at about the 50th floor, a guy would say come on in, what've you got? He'd be having lunch, and I'd tell him about the utilities fund." Ibid.

(23) "That was a very aggressive payout." Ibid.

(27–28) "What's the first bill a consumer is going to pay?" Interview with Rupert H. Johnson, Jr., by Marilyn Tobias, July 28, 2005.

(28) "How would you like to make money every time someone turns on his lights in the United States?" Interview with Richard C. Stoker by Marilyn Tobias, September 29, 2005.

(28) "He showed me how you really make a story come alive." Ibid.

(30) "…a hedge against what politicians might do." Russell Van Denburgh, "Fund Expects Strong Rally," *San Diego Union*, January 26, 1969.

(32–33) "played footsie" and other quotes from David Babson are in David Colbert, *Eyewitness to Wall Street* (New York: Broadway Books, 2001).

(39) "I never read research reports any-more. [I'm] a merchandise manager in a department store. I look for what's going to sell next year." Martin Mayer, *New Breed on Wall Street: The Young Men Who Make the Money Go* (New York: The Macmillan Company, 1969).

(41) "…but San Francisco was an attractive area." Interview with Rupert H. Johnson, Jr., by Marilyn Tobias, July 28, 2005.

(42) "I drove my dad's car." Harmon E. Burns from interview with Charles B. Johnson, Rupert H. Johnson, Jr., and Harmon E. Burns, July 11, 2006.

(42 & 44) "We had a chance to talk and it came across very clearly to me that Burns was a very solid citizen with good judgment. I developed a lot of confidence in him just from three or four hours driving with him." Charles B. Johnson in interview with Charles B. Johnson, Rupert H. Johnson, Jr., and Harmon E. Burns, July 11, 2006.

(44) "I was happy to get some new, younger blood on the management team, especially from the financial establishment back East." Harmon E. Burns in interview with Charles B. Johnson, Rupert H. Johnson, Jr., and Harmon E. Burns, July 11, 2006.

(45) "Usually the meeting was in Hawaii or in some fancy resort, but that year they had it in Williamsburg.… It rained, and it was just miserable, and everybody was down in the dumps." Charles B. Johnson from interview with Charles B. Johnson, Rupert H. Johnson, Jr., and Harmon E. Burns, July 11, 2006.

(48) "Charlie was interested in experimenting in ways that would give leverage to our core business, but only if it helped our mutual fund business." Interview with Richard C. Stoker by Marilyn Tobias, September 13, 2005.

(49) "We were saving paper clips from mail that people sent to us, sharpening small pencils and cutting envelopes we received to make scratch paper." and "It was the hardest thing I ever had to do." Earl Johnson from interview with Earl and Ann Johnson, July 12, 2006.

(50) "Don't waste money, don't spend money you don't have." Interview with Harmon E. Burns by Marilyn Tobias, July 28, 2005.

(50) "I was looking at the business to make sure that we were going to survive." Charles B. Johnson from interview with Charles B. Johnson, Rupert H. Johnson, Jr., and Harmon E. Burns, July 11, 2006.

(50) "You try to figure out a way to differentiate yourself in the mutual fund industry…and there aren't that many ways. It's so easy to copy a fund…. We thought the one thing we might be able to do to set us apart would be service to the shareholders and the brokers. That was one of the guiding features of the business plan." Interview with Harmon E. Burns by Marilyn Tobias, July 28, 2005.

(50) "It was really the strength of Charlie's will that got the company through that period." Harmon E. Burns from interview with Charles B. Johnson, Rupert H. Johnson, Jr., and Harmon E. Burns, July 11, 2006.

(51) "I think the future belongs to the full-load industry. Mutual funds are still sold, not bought, and a person is not going to buy unless a salesman is out there explaining the business, giving him reasons for investing in the funds." Lawrence A. Armour, "Beyond Redemption: Franklin Custodian's Johnson Looks Hopefully to the Future," *Barron's,* March 12, 1973.

(52) "…the IRA customer can switch from one fund to another with no tax consequences and no commissions." Also: "…because its seven funds present a wide spectrum.…" William Shepherd, "Swinging with the New IRA Plans," *BusinessWeek,* June 30, 1975.

(54) "The salespeople were adamantly against it. I think that as an organization we had faith that the market would come back." Harmon E. Burns from interview with Charles B. Johnson, Rupert H. Johnson, Jr., and Harmon E. Burns, July 11, 2006.

(57) "I remember he got so mad." Harmon E. Burns in interview with Charles B. Johnson, Rupert H. Johnson, Jr., and Harmon E. Burns, July 11, 2006.

(58) "…cash management vehicle." Joseph Nocera, *A Piece of the Action: How the Middle Class Joined the Money Class* (New York: Simon & Schuster, 1994).

(59) "…money market fund." Steve Massey, "Money Market Mogul Glen Johnson Cashed in 24 Years Ago by Making Bank Trust Officers Feel Special," *Pittsburgh Post-Gazette,* September 12, 1997.

(60) "It seems funny today, but nobody really could figure out where this business was going." Charles B. Johnson from interview with Charles B. Johnson, Rupert H. Johnson, Jr., and Harmon E. Burns, July 11, 2006.

(61) "You didn't have a broker/dealer to take their phone calls. So we had to have an ever-growing group of people to handle the calls." Harmon E. Burns from interview with Charles B. Johnson, Rupert H. Johnson, Jr., and Harmon E. Burns, July 11, 2006.

(61) "A lot of people thought we were a bank. They would bring a check, and they would ask for change back." Rupert H. Johnson, Jr., in interview with Charles B. Johnson, Rupert H. Johnson, Jr., and Harmon E. Burns, July 11, 2006.

(61) "We would make them go down to a bank and get a bank check." Charles B. Johnson in interview with Charles B. Johnson, Rupert H. Johnson, Jr., and Harmon E. Burns, July 11, 2006.

(65) "The downside risk is minimal, and the upside potential could be explosive." "The Funds Hope to Improve on 1977's Gain," *BusinessWeek,* December 26, 1977.

(69) "The group had a unique personality that reflected Andy's personality and approach." Harmon E. Burns from interview with Charles B. Johnson, Rupert H. Johnson, Jr., and Harmon E. Burns, July 11, 2006.

(70) SIDEBAR. "We didn't know anything about bonds when we started." Telephone interview with Rafael Costas, November 2, 2006.

(70) SIDEBAR. "We learned from the stories they told." Telephone interview with Thomas Walsh, November 2, 2006.

(70) SIDEBAR. "This was the best way to learn because there was no way to learn about the bond market without being entrenched in it." Telephone interview with Sheila Amoroso, November 2, 2006.

(72) "For most of their history, stock funds have been the dominant force among mutual funds. The record set by Franklin U.S. Government Securities Fund reflects investors' desire for high income with a high degree of safety." Franklin Templeton Investments, "Franklin U.S. Government Securities Fund Is Now the Largest Mutual Fund in the U.S., Except for a Few Big Money Market Funds," press release, March 14, 1985.

(73) "The process resulted in lots of errors." Frank J. Isola, "Notes regarding Franklin Templeton history," April 25, 2006. Personal correspondence with the authors.

(73) SIDEBAR. "He always had very good judgment, and I very much valued his insights and opinions." Charles B. Johnson in interview with Charles B. Johnson, Rupert H. Johnson, Jr., and Harmon E. Burns, July 11, 2006.

(74) "We were suddenly opening hundreds and sometimes more than a thousand accounts a day." Frank J. Isola, "Notes regarding Franklin Templeton history," April 25, 2006. Personal correspondence with the authors.

(77) "By that time I had worked with Harmon for seven years and I can't remember a time that I didn't agree with his judgment." Charles B. Johnson in interview with Charles B. Johnson, Rupert H. Johnson, Jr., and Harmon E. Burns, July 11, 2006.

(79) "He would come home from work late, and then run." Ann Johnson from interview with Charles B. Johnson, Ann Johnson and Jennifer Bolt, July 11, 2006.

(88) "I began to chuckle. I thought it had almost gotten to the point of being silly." "An Industry Veteran's View: 'The World Isn't Coming to an End,'" *Barron's,* November 9, 1987.

(94) "We're always looking.... As long as you can offer a rate of return higher than inflation, you are performing an investment service." Karen Southwick, "Franklin Resources' Amazing Growth—Assets under Management Hit $20 Billion," *San Francisco Chronicle,* March 31, 1986.

(98) "...one of the most exciting retail asset management marketplaces in Asia, and one that...holds much promise for the future." Report by Cerulli Associates, quoted in Karen Richardson, "Taiwan's Fund Industry Heats Up," *The Wall Street Journal,* September 12, 2002.

(99) "When you go into the Morgan Guaranty Trust Company, you never ask, 'Where's J. P. Morgan?'...When you come to Templeton International, it's a little out of date to say, 'Where's Templeton?' Ninety-five percent of the work is done by the 500 other people." "Funds with Personality," *St. Petersburg Times,* June 4, 1990.

(100) "We had wanted to diversify for some time." "But What about the Gander? Investors May Do Better in Franklin Resources' Stock Than in Its Newest Funds—If the Market Doesn't Falter," *Financial World [FW],* August 3, 1993.

(100) "...firms like Templeton's don't come on the market very often. He's got what we don't: a broad line of equity products, a fantastic track record and an international infrastructure. To survive in the next 10 years, we'll have to be global." "Biggest-Ever Merger of Mutual Funds, Franklin Pays Templeton $913 Million," *San Francisco Chronicle,* August 1, 1992.

(102) "I remember coming back from a trip to Europe on a Friday night, and Sir John said, 'Tomorrow morning you will meet your new owners.'" Telephone interview with Martin L. Flanagan, November 18, 2006.

(104) "...the two organizations fit like a hand in a glove..." "Templeton Sets Sale of Funds to Franklin," *The Wall Street Journal,* August 3, 1992.

(106) "Templeton was sold on reputation and track record." Telephone interview with Peter Jones, April 13, 2006.

(106) "Now people will stop asking me, 'What's going to happen to my investment when John Templeton dies?'" "Merger Creates Biggest Fund," *Austin American-Statesman,* August 1, 1992.

(107) "...a perfect fit...." Ibid.

(109) "You had these incredible mentors teaching you the business." Telephone interview with Jeffrey Everett, September 8, 2006.

(109) "...were expected to take care of themselves." Telephone interview with Martin L. Flanagan, November 18, 2006.

(110) "...has worked out very well." *The Globe and Mail,* July 18, 1996.

(110) "Every article written by the press focused on Franklin's strength in sales and distribution." Telephone interview with Peter Jones, April 13, 2006.

(111) "A financial advisor had to discover the company." Ibid.

(113) "...to bring our pricing in line...." Kalen Holliday, "Franklin to Raise Front-End Sales Fees on Funds," *American Banker,* Vol. 159, No. 54.

(113) "We've been hesitant about bringing out multiple class structures, but this recognizes a growing trend." Kathleen Pender, "Franklin Raises Loaded Question about Funds," *San Francisco Chronicle*, January 17, 1995.

(113 & 115) "We are no longer as blindly optimistic as we were." Howard Kapiloff, "Chastened Franklin Hangs Tough in Bank Sales," *American Banker*, Vol. 161, No. 56, March 22, 1996.

(115) "We will not be where we should be in the bank channel until we have B shares available. It's just too strong a pricing force through that distribution channel, and I think it cost us a lot in sales." Stephen Garmhausen, "Franklin Returns as Contender in Bank Fund Sales," *American Banker*, Vol. 163, No. 56, March 24, 1998.

(116) "We were a buyer of undervalued stocks. You do your homework. If you do the work and wait for the market to hand you a stock on the cheap, you'll come out all right." Telephone Interview with Michael Price, March 7, 2006.

(116) SIDEBAR. "...to buy a dollar for 50 cents...." Ibid.

(116–117) "...stalker of underperforming CEOs...." Andrew E. Serwer et al., "Mr. Price Is on the Line," *Fortune*, December 9, 1996.

(117) "You have to ask yourself why you're buying something when the smartest man on Wall Street is selling it." Ibid.

(117) SIDEBAR. "So what do you like?" Telephone interview with Michael Price, March 7, 2006.

(118) "Our whole focus was on the price to EBITDA....This ratio was very reasonable." Barry Henderson and

Lauren Young, "Rich Price for Price's Mutual Series Is Fair, Analysts Say," *Dow Jones Money Management Alert*, June 25, 1996.

(118) "We were operating off three separate shareholder accounting systems and attempting to make it appear transparent to the customer. Needless to say, our problems were many, and transparent it was not." Frank J. Isola, "Notes regarding Franklin Templeton history," April 25, 2006.

(123) "I see the world as an opportunity as political barriers to investing come down in different countries." Benjamin Ensor, "Charles Johnson, President and Chief Executive Officer, Franklin Resources," *Global Investor*, March 1, 1997.

(124) "...home country regulation, host country marketing...." "Unit Trust Management Groups Are Counting Down to October 1, D-Day for Europe-Wide Marketing," *Post Magazine*, September 21, 1989.

(126) "Banks had their own proprietary funds and we had no chance to take them head-on." Telephone interview with Hans Wisser, July 14, 2006.

(126) "That inspired and put pressure on other banks." Ibid.

(127) "...frustrated by the slowness of the UK authorities in allowing investment products to be priced, packaged and taxed in a way that is more appealing to foreign as well as to domestic investors." Douglas Adams, "SICAVS, OEICS or Traditional UK Unit Trusts? Investors in Mutual Funds Will Soon Have a Wider Choice," *The Independent* (London), February 3, 1996.

PAGE
NUMBER

(129) "...one of our goals was to educate the public about investment in our funds." Shiv Taneja, "Templeton's Maiden Fund in S'Pore Raises S$40M," *Business Times Singapore,* July 23, 1996.

(130) "...to create and locally register new mutual funds in Korea." "Templeton, Ssangyong Form Venture in Korea," *The Asian Wall Street Journal,* August 14, 1996.

(130–131) "Then I heard about foreign mutual funds coming into the market. I heard that they distribute risk and that they can invest worldwide. I need something secure like that.... I'm willing to pay the management fee these companies charge if the fund is managed correctly and they give me long-term security." Pui-wing Tam and In Kyung Kim, "Korea's Mutual-Fund Market Creaks Open— Investors to Gain Access to Wide Choice of Foreign-Managed Funds," *The Asian Wall Street Journal,* February 13, 1997.

(131) "...a lot of development in the industry will be local with many companies setting up joint ventures." Benjamin Ensor, "Charles Johnson, President and Chief Executive Officer, Franklin Resources," *Global Investor,* March 1, 1997.

(131) "We developed a strong personal relationship and brought Templeton in as a minority stakeholder in the first mutual fund in Sri Lanka." Telephone interview with Vijay Advani, August 22, 2006.

(131) "We talked about Russia, Poland and India. He was like a sponge, wanting to know all my experiences." Ibid.

PAGE
NUMBER

(133) "The regulator required us to have $10.7 million. I was paranoid they would shut us down." Ibid.

(133) "You had people handing out fliers for funds on street corners." Ibid.

(134) "India will be a good market if and when regulations are improved.... More and more of the bureaucratic barriers and red tape are coming down." Economist Intelligent Unit, "Room at the Top: Foreign Entrants Have Energised Mutual Funds in India, but the Industry Continues to Account for Only a Tiny Share of the Market Capitalisation of Listed Equity," *Business India Intelligence,* January 26, 2005.

(134) "That was the first time people in our office saw how humble he is, despite all that he has accomplished. He took time with each person. He told them what they were doing reminded him of his work to build Franklin 30 years earlier." Telephone interview with Vijay Advani, August 22, 2006.

(135) "It led to the rise of a middle class in Mexico, Argentina and Chile, which created excellent opportunities for Franklin Templeton." Ibid.

(135) "...wild times...." Telephone interview with Jed Plafker, July 25, 2006.

(135) "...a window of opportunity for mutual fund companies to team up with local banks and brokerage firms." Jonathan Friedland, "U.S., European Funds Are Starting to Target Latin America Region," *The Wall Street Journal Europe,* October 10, 1995.

(136) "We don't go in with a cookie-cutter approach.... You have to understand the local environment and determine how we can best position ourselves in those countries in terms of strategy, product development, target market, global products and international products." Ibid.

(136–137) "There's no reason why we can't duplicate in Russia what we have in the United States." Patricia Kranz, "Rushing to Russia," *BusinessWeek*, March 19, 1997.

(137) "We're happy to start off slowly in these countries [like India and Russia]. We'd rather wait and get it right. You can't turn on the light switch the first day you raise the money." "Templeton/Russia: New Fund Took Two Years to Plan," *Dow Jones News Service*, April 30, 1997.

(138) "...education is huge in these countries...." Ibid.

(138) SIDEBAR. "Bad times can be good times." Mark Mobius and Stephen Fenichell, *Passport to Profits: Why the Next Investment Windfalls Will Be Found Abroad and How to Grab Your Share* (New York: Warner Books, 1999).

(138) "Nobody has checks in Russia.... There was no way to distribute the dividends." Telephone interview with Charles B. Johnson, September 19, 2006.

(142–143) "...irrational exuberance...." Joseph E. Stiglitz, *The Roaring Nineties: A New History of the World's Most Prosperous Decade* (New York: W.W. Norton & Company, 2003).

(143) "I buy these stocks because I live in a competitive universe, and I can't beat my benchmarks without them.... You either participate in this mania, or you go out of business." Joseph Nocera, "Do You Believe? How Yahoo! Became a Blue Chip," *Fortune*, July 7, 1999, reprinted in David Colbert, *Eyewitness to Wall Street* (New York: Broadway Books, 2001).

(143) "I don't understand. People talk about the industry, and we never get mentioned. It is like we fell off the earth." Harmon E. Burns quoted in interview with Jennifer Bolt, January 20, 2006.

(145) "I have been around for a long time, and I remember the Nifty 50 in the 1960s, which were the large growth stocks—computers, pharmaceutical companies and so on. Everybody jumped in after them, and then they crashed." Charles B. Johnson quoted in interview with Gregory E. Johnson, June 6, 2006.

(147) "The question we ask is: 'Where are the bargains?' If there are no bargains, then we are not interested." Marissa Lague, "Funds Guru Speaks out—Franklin Investment Services," *South China Morning Post*, November 6, 1994.

(147) "If [Mobius] didn't exist, the emerging markets world would have to invent him." "Power Brokers: The SmartMoney 30," *SmartMoney*, September 1, 1997.

(148) "There is no way to mince words about the fund's performance." Barry Henderson, "Trying Times: At Franklin Foreign Exposure, Lagging Performance Burden a Fund Giant," *Barron's*, October 5, 1998.

(150) "That is unacceptable." Telephone interview with Charles B. Johnson, September 19, 2006.

(152) "…because we are beginning to realize the benefits of our conversion onto a single shareholder system." Charles B. Johnson, email to all employees, January 14, 1999.

(152) "We all need to focus our efforts on continually improving customer service, streamlining our business processes, controlling expenses and ensuring our resources are allocated to those activities that best service our clients." Ibid.

(153) "Many employees that I spoke to thought the cost-cutting initiatives signaled the end of the company." Telephone interview with Charles B. Johnson, October 16, 2006.

(155) "We helped the consultants, and they helped us get into the 401(k) market we'd been boxed out of." Telephone interview with Norman R. Frisbie, Jr., September 29, 2006.

(157) "…the best-known market guru, and she's been right for a long time." Eileen Glanton, "Influential Strategist Sends Stocks Tumbling," *Associated Press Newswires*, March 28, 2000.

(157) "For the first time in a decade, our model portfolio is no longer recommending an overweighted position in technology. Many of the technology shares were given the respect they deserve over the last 18 months, and are no longer undervalued." Ibid.

(158) "You need a better one-year [performance] number before you start to see any real shift in flows. We are getting very close to that stage." Gregory E. Johnson quoted in

Yuka Hayashi, "Value Picker Franklin Now a Value Play?," *Dow Jones Newswires*, August 23, 2000.

(161) "…demonstrate to the world that when we said we were not for sale, we were not for sale." "Franklin Resources Not for Sale, CEO Says," *Reuters News*, October 25, 2000.

(166) "We have emerged from September 11 with a renewed sense of purpose, yet we live constantly with the memories of the colleagues and friends we lost that day." Anne Tatlock, "Letter," Fiduciary Trust International, September 11 Information & Archive, www.ftci.com/ftci_9-11-01/letter.html. This quote has been used in slightly different forms in several Franklin Templeton publications.

(168) "All of their faces suddenly came to me." James M. Clash and Rob Wherry, "Shattered, Not Broken; Fiduciary Trust's Backup Plan Worked," *Forbes*, October 15, 2001.

(170) "Clients were calling us just to hear the sound of our voices and to offer condolences." Ibid.

(170) "She was strong, but after one family left we could see the strain." Telephone interview with Martin L. Flanagan, November 18, 2006.

(172) "Looking back, one of the things that continues to resonate in my mind from that day and the days that followed is the way that our employees around the world and especially in New York City responded, how we helped each other through that very difficult time. It was an unforgettable display of humanity." Gregory E. Johnson, "Reflecting on 9/11," email to employees, September 12, 2006.

(178) "An already difficult year for the financial markets was exacerbated by the
events of September 11." Franklin
Resources, Inc., *2001 Annual Report*.

(178) "…very focused on cost containment."
John Shipman, "Franklin Resources
Execs Outline Cost-Cutting
Measures," *Dow Jones News Service*,
October 25, 2001.

(179) "…we have been in positive sales all
year long, including August when a
lot of people weren't." Neil Martin,
"Value in Vogue: Widely Criticized in
the late 1990s, Franklin Resources Is
Back in Style," *Barron's*, October 7,
2002.

(180) "…a mutual fund revolution inspired
by the example of the U.S. is sweeping through India, transforming markets in its wake." "Mutual Fund Boom
Sweeps through India," *Financial
Times*, September 20, 1999.

(180) "He gave time and encouragement
to people. He never demoralized
people. He encouraged incremental
progress. He was always looking to
the long term." Telephone interview
with Vijay Advani, July 21, 2006.

(181) "…swiftly emerging from the shadow
of the once dominant public sector
fund managers." "Mutual Fund Boom
Sweeps through India," *Financial
Times*, September 20, 1999.

(181) "There is no excuse for my actions
in any way, and I make none. I take
full responsibility." George Anders,
"Succession Drama: Groomed to
Lead, Fund Clan's Scion Veered into
Trouble," *The Wall Street Journal*,
November 18, 2003.

(183) "…we prefer not to go the redemption-
fee route because it reduces flexibility
for investors who are not timers…

but we will go that route if we conclude that it is the best route for all
shareholders." Dan Culloton, "Let
the Times Beware," *Morningstar.com*,
August 18, 2000. Available at
http://news.morningstar.com.

(184) "…20 percent of stocks lost 60
percent or more of their value, not
even one-tenth of one percent of
all funds had the same type of loss."
Eric Garland, "Half-Speed Ahead:
The Era of Full-Throttle Growth for
Mutual Funds May Be Over. But as
Franklin Resources Executive Greg
Johnson Explains, the Basic Vehicle Is
Still Running Well," *Financial Planning*,
May 1, 2003.

(185) "…payments and other
inducements…." Yuka Hayashi,
"Spitzer's Probe Sheds New Light on
Market Timing in Funds," *Dow Jones
News Service*, September 3, 2003.

(185) "…sully the record of what has been
a reputable and responsible fund
family." Dan Culloton, "Scandal
Sullies Franklin Templeton's
Reputation," *Morningstar.com*,
February 26, 2004.

(190) "…were mainly concerned about
relative performance." Harry
Marmer, *Benefits Canada*, April 2006.

(192) "It was a very down-to-earth board."
Telephone interview with Richard
Frank, May 3, 2006.

(192) "That was a real endorsement." Ibid.

(192) "We talked to a large pension fund
and to an insurance company." Ibid.

(193) "Some people were afraid that
we would be swallowed up in a
big bureaucracy, but that didn't
materialize." Ibid.

PAGE
NUMBER

(196) "We have to change our thinking from a mutual fund company to an investment management organization." Gregory E. Johnson quoted in Jon Boilard and Kelly Dubois, "Roundtable Discussion With OOP: Presidents Are Energizing the Company," *Portrait Express,* March 31, 2000.

(197) "Through research, we found that very few financial advisors or investors had a complete understanding of what Franklin Templeton Investments had to offer. But when we presented them with the multi-manager concept, it resonated and increased their estimation of the firm." John Greer quoted in Jon Boilard and Kelly Dubois, "Roundtable Discussion With OOP: Presidents Are Energizing the Company," *Portrait Express,* March 31, 2000.

(199) "Sounds like a great job." Charles B. Johnson in interview with Charles B. Johnson, Ann Johnson and Jennifer Bolt, July 11, 2006.

(200) "...enables quick decision-making, allows groups to leverage core capabilities and resources, and broadens the opportunities available to all employees." Gregory E. Johnson, email to all employees, September 8, 2005.

(201) "We continue to deliver very strong, consistent relative performance from our portfolio teams. Our sales and marketing groups continue to build relationships around the globe. And finally, we continue to deliver excellent service to our clients and customers." Gregory E. Johnson, videoconference with all employees, December 13, 2005.

(201) "Our vision, as you know, is to be the premier global investment management organization." Ibid.

PAGE
NUMBER

(205) "...access to the investment world unlike any other product up to that time." "Q&A with Charles B. Johnson" in *Investor Topics,* Franklin Templeton newsletter, Summer 2006.

(207) "Our sensations being very much fixed to the moment, we are apt to forget that more moments are to follow the first, and consequently that a man should arrange his conduct to suit the whole of a life." Benjamin Vaughn quoted in Benjamin Franklin, *The Autobiography of Benjamin Franklin,* online version of Charles W. Eliot edition, published by P.F. Collier & Sons (1909) at www.books.eserver.org/nonfiction/franklin.

Index

Our Franklin Templeton employees and friends lost on September 11, 2001, are commemorated on pages 174–175. Their names are included in this index only if they appear elsewhere in the text.

HAPPY 300TH BIRTHDAY, BEN

Born on January 17, 1706, Ben Franklin offered
perspective that has stood the test of time.

Others saw lightning—Ben saw electricity. They saw a penny saved—he saw a
penny earned. Ben Franklin saw things with a unique perspective. So do we. Ours
is derived from over 50 years of experience, a world-class manager structure
and offices in 29 countries. This perspective allows us to spot investment
opportunities that others might miss. It's one reason we've become a leading
investment manager in the U.S. and around the world.

FRANKLIN TEMPLETON
INVESTMENTS

< GAIN FROM OUR PERSPECTIVE® >

Franklin Templeton Distributors, Inc., One Franklin Parkway, San Mateo, CA 94403.

Franklin Templeton celebrated Benjamin Franklin's
300th birthday in January 2006. A citizen of the world
and ardent patriot, Franklin believed that with persistence and perspective most individuals could achieve
greater prosperity.